"America is great because America is good,
and if America ceases to be good,
she will cease to be great."

MAKING
AMERICA
GOOD
AGAIN

*The Last Will and Testament
of a Country Preacher*

DANIEL E. JOHNSON

"Dan Johnson was my pastor during the formative years of my life. As a model and example, his influence in my ministry is unsurpassed. A strong communicator, he has been a favorite pulpit guest in churches I have pastored."

–Rev. Dale Oquist
Peoples Church
Fresno, California

Contents

Foreword

One chilly afternoon I stood at Plymouth Rock and imagined a similar day in 1620 when a small group of Pilgrims landed here. Who were these strangers and why had they come? A book on the history of the United States, widely used in our public schools, would shed some light, I thought, on the questions I posed—but as it turned out would also identify one of the reasons for the mess we're in. "Impelling curiosity," the author wrote, "was one of the prime forces that drove adventuresome Europeans to sail westward across the uncharted Atlantic to come by surprise upon a great wilderness later called America."

Impelling curiosity? William Bradford and George Carver, leaders of the Pilgrim community, would not have agreed. Curiosity was hardly a sufficient motivation to leave comfortable homes in familiar surroundings and sail unfriendly seas in little wooden boats. A better explanation is found in the solemn declaration to which they had affixed their signatures, establishing a commonwealth, "to the glory of God and advancement of the Christian faith." In fact, the Pilgrims constituted a church, and

the voyage to the new continent was literally a church reloca-
tion, a church plant.

This generation is sadly unaware of the narrative because we
have intentionally ignored our history and dismissed our founding documents as irrelevant, if not myth and superstition. Our
history books have undergone systematic revision in an attempt
to downplay or camouflage our forefathers' Christian commitment. The facts show that these hardy souls came to America
because they were determined to establish a beachhead from
which the gospel of Jesus Christ could be taken to the ends of
the earth.

Our nation was established by men and women who possessed an abiding faith in God, people who loved the Bible. As
students of the Reformation that swept Europe in the sixteenth
century, they had been influenced by the teachings of John Calvin, Martin Luther and others, giants of the faith who taught that
man, a sinner by nature, can be regenerated and transformed by
the gospel. Teaching the sovereignty of God and the lordship
of Christ and the authority of the Bible, the reformers realized
that spiritual growth depends on making it possible for common
people to read the Scriptures for themselves. This would require
two innovative and radical social changes: the translation of the
Bible into the language of the man on the street and the education of the people so they could read the Bible and understand
what they were reading.

This is the book that made America, the single book our forefathers brought with them when they came. They were Bible
people, poring over the Scriptures by day and by night, searching
for wisdom, seeking answers as to how to build a community, a
nation. Never in the history of the world, with the exception of
Israel, had a nation been established on such a foundation. "In
colonial America," Russell Kirk comments, "everyone with the
rudiments of schooling knew one book thoroughly, the Bible.
And the Old Testament mattered as much as the New."

In a document that became the first state constitution and was later the prototype for the Constitution of the United States, Pastor Thomas Hooker called for an "orderly and decent government according to God." William Penn, a devout Quaker, stated his desire to establish Pennsylvania as a "holy experiment" in religious and political freedom. The commitment of these settlers to establish a "covenant" nation permeated every aspect of early American life. The story is told in their documents and in their laws, in their homes and schools and churches.

John Winthrop, the Puritans' strongest leader, on the deck of the ship Arbella, halfway between England and Cape Cod, in the year 1630, reminded his fellow-voyagers how they had made a covenant with the God of Israel:

> We must delight in each other, make others' conditions our own, rejoice together, mourn together, labor and suffer together, always having before our eyes our commission and community in the work, our community as members of the same body . . . We shall find that the God of Israel is among us when ten of us shall be able to resist a thousand of our enemies, when He shall make us a praise and a glory . . . For we must consider that we shall be as a city upon a hill.

French diplomat and political scientist Alexis de Tocqueville came to this young country in 1831 to study our prisons and penitentiaries. He traveled widely over several months, talking to people, observing our way of life, examining records.. Upon returning home he wrote *Democracy in America* in which he makes some very interesting observations. He concluded that It was America's moral order that sustained America's social order and that order was based on moral convictions. "For the Americans," Tocqueville found, "the ideas of Christianity and liberty are so completely mingled that it is almost impossible to get them to conceive of one without the other."

A quote often used by politicians and preachers to spice up a sermon or speech has been attributed to Tocqueville, but it is not certain he said it. It is not found in *Democracy in America* or in any of his other writings. But because it is not unlike other things he said and is so insightful and instructive, it is worth noting:

> I searched for the greatness and genius of America in her commodious harbors and her ample rivers—and it was not there . . . in her fertile fields and boundless forests—and it was not there . . . in her rich mines and her vast world commerce—and it was not there. Not until I went into the churches and heard her pulpits aflame with righteousness did I understand the secret of her genius and power. *America is great because America is good, and if America ceases to be good, she will cease to be great.*

Of one thing we can be sure: righteousness exalts a nation, but sin is a reproach. Winthrop warned, "For if we deal falsely with our God and cause Him to hide His face from us, we shall become a story and by-word among the nations."

Well, where are we today? "We can shoot rockets into space but we can't cure anger or discontent," argues John Steinbeck. Solzhenitsyn described our time as "a world split apart."

> Jacques Ellul has spoken of the "betrayal" of the West by a corrupted intelligentsia; Philip Rieff has spoken of the "elaborate act of suicide" carried out by intellectuals as they have mutilated the culture by destroying the possibility of authority; Carl Henry has spoken of the "end" of the West. Richard Weaver has spoken of its dissolution; Emil Brunner has spoken of its "progressive estrangement" from its Christian base and its movement toward nihilism; Robert

Hilbrunner has spoken of the "indefinable unease" that haunts the modern spirit.

Thos. Oden, *Beyond Modernity*

So how did we allow this estrangement from our roots, this betrayal, to alter our nation's course? How did we talk ourselves into this trap of bartering our heritage for a mess of pottage? By what circuitous route did we become a nation adrift, beset by violence in our homes, in our schools, and on our streets? How did we get into this fix where we now find ourselves reeling under the weight of rebellion against God with its inevitable consequences: corruption in government, scandals in business, overcrowded prisons, dysfunctional families, broken homes? Even as I write these chapters, angry waves of anti-Christian venom pour onto the shore. The rapidity with which the attacks are coming is sobering. Our heritage is being stolen in broad daylight. Academia is complicit, the media is compliant, and the people are asleep. "An astonishing and horrible thing has been committed in the land: the prophets prophesy falsely, the priests rule by their own power; and My people love to have it so. But what will you do in the end?" (Jer. 5:30, 31). Listen to Hugh Hewitt of the American Alliance Defense Fund: "If it is up to the opposition, there will be no trace of the Christian heritage upon which our Founding Fathers established this country." He notes the threats Christian chaplains are facing in the United States military and levels a warning which must not go unheeded.

Today the darkness deepens. The suddenness with which moral barriers have fallen is stunning. The speed and velocity with which the goal posts are shifting leave us breathless. Behavior, lifestyles, practices which were a legal impossibility only short years ago are now accepted, even compulsory—and it is a crime to dissent. "That which was once condemned is now celebrated," said Dr. Al Mohler, "and refusing to celebrate is now condemned."

Atop the tallest building in Washington, D.C., are these words *Laus Deo* –English, "God be praised." The elevator that once carried 800,000 tourists a year to the top of the Washington Monument is broken, now closed indefinitely. We are told that fifteen million dollars can't fix it. As a nation, we face challenges that money cannot solve. We are going as Jeremiah said, "backwards and not forwards" (Jer. 7:24). We eat but are not satisfied (Lev 26:26). We are technologically superior to our parents but morally and spiritually empty—and the elevator's not working.

William D. Watkins, writing in *The New Absolutes*, says:

> Sometimes on still, warm southern nights, I step into my backyard and look into the night sky. I peer into the star-studded dark and wonder what America's fate will be. Will we gain the vision and the will to turn back the night enveloping us? Or will we continue to imbibe the new absolutes? At times I feel hopeful. On some nights, though, there's a chill in the air.

Twenty years ago, after several years of research, I wrote a book recounting our history, examining our roots, chronicling the events that have brought us to this moment. The week *Come Home America* was published, I went to Washington, D.C., and hand-delivered a copy to every member of the United States Congress. Then I went back and forth across the country, sounding the alarm, reminding the people of who we are, where we came from, and the price that was paid for our freedoms. Since it was first published, other challenges have arisen: the threat of militant Islam, the ongoing struggle for the survival of the State of Israel, the rise of a new, aggressive atheism, and the unabated slide toward the moral abyss.

This revised and expanded edition of *Come Home America* brings together excepts from *Aim for the Children* and other out-of-print writings by the author and is sent forth with the hope that its reading may drive us to our knees in fervent prayer for divine intervention in the 21st century. The first chapter is a thumbnail sketch of who we are and identifies the building blocks upon which our republic rests. This is followed by a discussion of the State of Israel and the importance of our national commitment to its survival and prosperity, believing that our own survival may hinge, in part, on that commitment. Then we examine the twists and turns that account for the kind of country we are today.

Of particular significance is the chapter on education, *Why Johnny Can't Read*. There is a reason for the widespread illiteracy among the population, and it is critical that we understand its moral, spiritual, and intellectual implications. *The Sixties and Beyond* casts light on the cultural milieu through which we are passing. Where is the church in all this? That discussion is required reading. *Out of the Night* is a poignant retelling of Nina Altmon's nightmare in Hitler's world, a reminder of what happened when the church in Germany was silent. Finally, after slogging through the rehearsal of the best of times and the worst of times in the story of our country, your spirits will be revived in the last chapter to learn that "we are not slouching toward Gomorrah, we are marching to Zion."

1

WE THE PEOPLE

O ver 1,500 of its 2,200 passengers were lost when the Titanic sank on April 15, 1912, en route to New York from Southampton, on its maiden voyage. Rabbi Daniel Lapin asks intriguing questions in *America's Real War:* "What exact moment condemned the Titanic? Was it the design of the lifeboat systems? Was it the choice of material used in the hull? Was it actually the moment the ship struck the iceberg?"

He goes on to say that the sinking of the great ship makes "a perfect metaphor for the expected demise of a great and apparently invulnerable enterprise." Referring to the United States, he cites some unsettling trends—violence in schools, babies found in dumpsters, assaults on traditional values, rejection of time-honored standards of decency and virtue—then asks, "When did we hit the iceberg?"

We have the largest educational system in the world, but don't know what to teach. We have banished God from the public square, but don't know who or what to put in His place. We have relaxed the old Christian morality, but don't know how to stanch the bleeding. One writer noted that we are suffering from what may be a terminal illness: alienation from all fixed truth. The foundations are cracked, the edges are frayed, the whole edifice may be coming down, and the extent of our moral decay is our very indifference to it.

Is America at the crossroads or did we long ago pass that juncture, make some bad choices, and are we now heading in the wrong direction? Have we collided with an iceberg, but don't know it? Are the waters even now rushing into the watertight compartments down below? If so, why does the dancing continue in the first-class ballroom?

Perhaps we've lost our way, forgotten who we are. In terms of history, laws, orientation and governance from the beginning, we are a Christian nation, as China is a Communist nation and Italy, Catholic. India is largely Hindu and Saudi Arabia, Muslim. "The general principles on which the fathers achieved independence were the general principles of Christianity," said John Adams.

Theodore Roosevelt declared: "The teachings of the Bible are so interwoven and entwined with our whole civic and social life that it would be literally impossible for us to figure to ourselves what life would be if these teachings were removed." Similar statements have been made over the years by presidents of both parties—Woodrow Wilson, Herbert Hoover, Truman, Nixon— and other leaders, by historians, Christians and non-Christians alike. Michael Medved, national talk show host and columnist spoke for many Jewish leaders: "The framers may not have mentioned Christianity in the Constitution but they presuppose America's unequivocal identity as a Christian nation."

Why is this important? Former president Obama said, "We are a nation of citizens who are bound by ideas and a set of values." But where did these ideas originate, what gave birth to this set of values? Who are we? What are the taproots of this national enterprise? One thing is certain, people with no history have no future.

> We are a nation conceived in liberty,
>> not an accident of history;
>> we know who we are, and why we're here.
> We built a city upon a hill,
>> poured tea in Boston Harbor,
>> took a midnight ride with Paul Revere,
>> and fired the shot heard round the world.
> We fought at Lexington and Concord to be free,
>> at Antietam, Bunker Hill and Ft. Sumter
>> to save the Union.
> We fought a Ypres and Verdun,
>> and piled the bodies high at Austerlitz and Waterloo.
> We shed blood on the sands of Iwo Jima,
>> and in the jungles of Guadalcanal.
> We scaled the cliffs with grappling hooks—
>> We are the boys of Pointe du Hoc.
> We waded rice fields of the Me Kong Delta,
>> and fought our way to Pyongyang.
> We are Washington praying at Valley Forge—
>> Patrick Henry: "If this be treason . . ."
> Nathan Hale with but one life to lose for his country—
>> William Lloyd Garrison,
>> writing in his anti-slavery newspaper:
>> "I will not equivocate—I will not excuse—I will not
>> retreat a single inch—and I will be heard."
> We are Robert Frost who took the road less traveled—
>> Neil Armstrong: "That's one small step for man . . ."
>> Billy Graham: "The Bible says . . ."
> Ronald Reagan: "Mr. Gorbachev, tear down this wall."
> We are mothers and fathers, boys and girls, artists and
>> craftsmen.

We are doctors and lawyers, teachers and statesmen, preachers and farmers. We are airline pilots and bus drivers; accountants, nurses, firemen and legislators. We are the United States Marines.

We survived the Boston Massacre, the Civil War, two World Wars, the Great Depression, the madness of the Sixties, some bad politicians, 9/11—and we're not going anywhere.

We are entombed in a watery grave at Pearl Harbor; buried in Flanders Fields, in Arlington, and at Gettysburg.

We are the unknown solider—but known to God. We lie beneath small crosses in a thousand cemeteries where prayers are made, tears are shed, and flowers are left on Memorial Day.

We know who we are—WE THE PEOPLE—One Nation Under God.

What can we learn about the character of the people who built this country? What Providence guided them in forming a government that affords its people such lavish opportunities? Our neglected history books chronicle the events leading up to the writing and ratification of the Constitution.

Princeton University (originally College of New Jersey) had gone through four presidents in a relatively short period of time. After an extended search for someone qualified spiritually and academically, they found their man in Scotland, a Presbyterian clergyman by the name of John Witherspoon. After some hesitation, Witherspoon accepted the assignment, brought his family to New Jersey, and began writing one of the great chapters in our early history.

A remarkable revival occurred in the third and fourth years of his administration. We know much about the caliber of the men who came out of the college following these years. Under the leadership of John Witherspoon, Princeton University produced one president, two vice presidents, 10 members of the president's cabinet, 12 senators, 29 members of the House of Representatives, three justices of the Supreme Court, 12 state governors and nine of the 55 founding members of our country.

Out of that environment came a young man who would leave his mark on history. Upon graduation, James Madison remained behind for a year and a half to study under the personal tutelage of President Witherspoon, studying theology, Hebrew and the Law of Moses. Who could have known—but God—that the young man was being uniquely prepared to guide in the writing of the Constitution of the United States.

At the young age of 35, James Madison was one of the 55 delegates to the Constitutional Convention in Philadelphia in 1787. All but three were church members, at a time when church membership meant something. Delegates came from all 13 colonies and labored from May until September—and it was never easy. Nothing like this had ever been done before and each participant had his own ideas as to how to formulate a document uniting separate states in one federal government.

By mid-summer, the convention had reached an impasse. The delegates had come from North and South, from colonies large and small, each member quite certain as to how best to proceed. One morning as temperatures rose and tempers flared, Benjamin Franklin, at 81 the oldest member of the delegation, rose to remind his colleagues of God's sovereign protection during the recent Revolutionary War:

> In the beginning of the contest with Britain, when we were sensible with danger, we had daily prayers in this room for divine protection. Our prayers, sir, were heard, and they were graciously answered. All of us who were engaged in that struggle must have observed frequent instances of a superintending Providence in our favor.

The revered Franklin pressed on, "And have we now forgotten this powerful Friend or do we imagine we no longer need His assistance?" With determined boldness, the great statesman continued, making this impassioned plea to the president of the convention, George Washington:

> I have lived, sir, a long time, and the longer I live the more convincing proofs I see of this truth that God governs in the affairs of men. And if a sparrow cannot fall to the ground without His notice, is it probable than an empire can rise without His aid? I, therefore, beg leave, to move that henceforth prayers employing the assistance of Heaven and its blessing on our deliberations be held in this assembly every morning before we proceed with business.

Roger Sherman of Connecticut seconded Franklin's motion for prayer, and Edmond Jennings Randolph of Virginia proposed that a sermon be preached on Independence Day—July 4.

Deliberations were suspended on June 28, and for the next three days the delegates fasted and prayed. When they returned on July 2, contention had been replaced by a spirit of collegiality. The deadlock broken, the representatives went on to write the Constitution, tying together 13 colonies in one indissoluble bond called the United States of America.

"There is no country in the whole world in which the Christian religion retains a greater influence over the souls of men than in America," wrote a Frenchman who came calling in 1831. The religious aspect of the country was the first thing that struck his attention. He found that the reason for this country's success was a sense of morality generated by the religious life of the people.

After nine months in the United States, Alexis de Tocqueville returned to France and in 1835 and published *Democracy in America*, in which he wrote, "I do not know whether all Americans have a sincere faith in their religion—for who can search the human heart?—but I am certain that they hold it to be indispensable to the maintenance of republican institutions. This opinion is not peculiar to a class of citizens or to a party, but it belongs to the whole nation and to every rank of society."

Tocqueville found that "the ideas of Christianity and liberty are so completely mingled that it is almost impossible to get them to conceive of one without the other; it is not a question with them of sterile beliefs bequeathed by the past and vegetating rather than living in the depths of the soul."

The French visitor found this astounding since in Europe church leaders often used the church to gain political power. As a result, the Christian religion was disdained by Europeans, and the clergy were seen as allies of the government, which at that time in Europe was often a tyrannical monarchy that controlled and enslaved the common people. It was different in America, Tocqueville found. A faith had forged a union out of a handful of diverse states, and that faith was Christianity. The book that made the nation great was the Bible.

The following paragraph is worth a very careful reading—and rereading. It is from *The Roots of American Order* by Russell Kirk, author of thirty books, who spent his life in the thick of many of the literary and political struggles of our time:

> The roots of order twist back to the Hebrew perceptions of a purposeful moral existence under God. They extend to the philosophical and political self-awareness of the old Greeks. They are nurtured by the Roman experience of law and social organization. They are entwined with the Christian understanding of human duties and human hopes, of man redeemed. They are quickened by the medieval custom, learning and value. They come from the ground of English liberty under law, so painfully achieved. They are secured by a century and a half of community in colonial America. They benefit from the

debates of the eighteenth century. They approach the surface through Declaration and Constitution. They emerge full of life from the ordeal of the Civil War. We need to understand where these thick roots and social order may be found. One of the more pressing perils of our time is that people may be cut off from their roots in culture and community.

The tendency to separate the culture from its roots is gaining momentum. Little by little this chipping away at the foundations goes on. On what grounds did the Supreme Court rule prayer illegal in public schools? Did our Founding Fathers intend for the Establishment Clause to be used to make the Ten Commandments something odious, even dangerous?

On the very day they completed their work in Philadelphia, the Continental Congress passed the Northwest Ordinance. This document was drafted to provide guidance to the new territories—Ohio, Illinois, Indiana, Michigan and beyond. Why is this significant? Because this ordinance states that "religion, morality, and civility, being necessary to good government and the happiness of mankind, schools and the means of education shall forever be encouraged." Note that this government document made it a law for "religion," which the delegates considered to be Christianity, to be taught in all educational institutions through the territories.

Teach religion and morality? What about separation of church and state? Doesn't our Constitution forbid religious instruction? The writers of this ordinance didn't think so, and many of them had helped frame the Constitution. It was never their intention to separate Christian teaching and practices from public life.

The actual wording of what is mislabeled the Establishment Clause reads: "Congress shall make no law respecting an establishment of religion, or prohibiting the free exercise thereof."

That statement simply means that lawmakers cannot decree

a national religion. They had left the old country to escape that kind of tyranny. On the very day Congress adopted the First Amendment, its members voted to install congressional chaplains and to make official days of thanksgiving and prayer. If Congress had meant to separate this government from God and the Bible, it surely would not have voted to participate in such obviously religious activities.

The phrase "separation of church and state," which is cited so frequently today, is not part of the Constitution. In fact, it is not found in any official government document. It was used only once, in a letter written by president Thomas Jefferson to a group of Christians who had heard a rumor that a certain denomination was going to become the official state religion of the United States. The Baptist Association of Danbury, Connecticut, wrote to the president expressing their concern, and received the following reply on January 1, 1802, assuring them this would not happen:

> I contemplate with solemn reverence that act of the whole American people which declared that their legislature should "make no law respecting an establishment of religion or prohibiting the free exercise thereof" thus building a wall of separation between church and state.

The rumor died away and the president's letter was lost and remained in obscurity for 76 years. No one had placed much significance in Jefferson's phrase until it reappeared in the 1878 case of *Reynolds v. United States*. At that point, the Supreme Court justices cited Jefferson's entire letter and used it to uphold—not limit—Christian practices in government institutions.

Once again the matter was dropped until in 1947 when the Supreme Court took the phrase out of context. They did not acknowledge the fact that Jefferson made it clear he was talking solely about the establishment of a state church, and nothing more, when he stated that there is a wall of separation between church and state. The Court, however, citing no case precedents, ruled that the Founding Fathers wanted a strict separation of religion from government.

The Supreme Court has since used the phrase repeatedly in its decisions. As a result, Americans have assumed that the United States Constitution separates government from all religious teaching and practice. The Supreme Court continues to ignore the intentions of our early leaders and on June 25, 1962, for the first time in our history struck down school prayer, equating the word "church" in the First Amendment with religious activity of any kind, making prayer illegal and unconstitutional in the public schools of the United States.

What was the offensive prayer students were reciting in their classrooms? It was a simple 22-word petition that doesn't even mention the name of Jesus: "Almighty God, we acknowledge our dependence upon Thee, and we beg Thy blessings upon us, our parents, our teachers and our country."

We've come a long way from those simpler times when we saw things clearly, when Princeton University, for example, stated in its rule book: "Cursed is all learning that is contrary to the cross of Christ."

Could we have imagined the price we would pay for having embraced a scholarship that is contrary to the cross of Christ? The superintendent of a large suburban school in Minneapolis called the local pastors together, stood before them grim-faced and said, "Gentlemen, from where I sit, I can smell the rotting fiber of our society. I see things happening in the lives of our children that brought the Roman Empire to ruin. Unless we do something about this, and do it soon, our children will grow up in an America which bears no resemblance to what we grew up in."

The Lynde and Harry Bradley Foundation made a detailed study of our country, where we've been and where we're headed. Their findings were included in *The Bradley Project on*

6/2008

America's Identity.

"America is facing an identity crisis," the study argued. "The next generation of Americans will know less than their parents know about our history and founding ideals. And many Americans are more aware of what divides us than of what unites us. The Bradley Project made a striking observation, and issued a warning:

> America is unique among nations in being founded not on a common ethnicity, but on a set of ideals. Ethnicity perpetuates itself by the fact of birth. But a nation founded on an idea starts anew with each new generation and with each new group of immigrants. Knowing what America stands for is not a genetic inheritance. It must be learned, both by the next generation and by those who come here. In this way, a nation founded on an idea is inherently fragile.

How is it fragile? Because "historical ignorance, civic neglect, and social fragmentation may achieve what no foreign conqueror could." Dumbed down, ignoring our history, flying blind, we are witnessing the most radical social transformation seen in our lifetime. "The analogy between the decadence of ancient civilizations," Russell Kirk writes, "and the decadence of our own culture is strikingly, dreadfully true."

Natan Sharansky recounts his experience in the Soviet prison system. For his part in helping Soviet Jews emigrate to Israel, he was incarcerated for nine years, much of it in solitary confinement. In *Fear No Evil*, he tells how a Bible somehow found its way into his prison cell, shedding light on his bleak existence. Reading the Hebrew Scriptures, Sharansky learned that the Jews had a history. They didn't come from nowhere but were part of an unfolding drama reaching back through the centuries; they were not alone. Sharansky said that he made a profound discovery, one that would sustain him through the years of deprivation, punishment and pain. "The minute you have an identity," he said, "you are a free person."

Identity and freedom are indissoluble. Before a people can be enslaved, they must be anesthetized. The Killing Fields of Cambodia were impossible until the intelligentsia, the professionals, the teachers and ministers were dispensed with. The gods are dethroned and the temples desecrated because dictators cannot abide dissent.

"If we forget what we did, we won't know who we are," said Ronald Reagan in his farewell address to the American people. "I am warning of the eradication of the American memory that could result, ultimately, in erosion of the American spirit."

Balint Vazsonyi, Hungarian-born historian and world renowned concert pianist, writes in *America's 30-Years War*, "The elimination of the nation's true history, expertly practiced in the Soviet Union and the Third Reich, guarantees commissars an uncontested field as they bring generations with blanks instead of history in their heads. Those blank areas can be filled with anything the commissars invent. There are no beacons of the past, no common orientation, no grid of reference to contradict the propaganda. That is why America's founding documents have been removed from the classroom. That is why civics classes have disappeared along with George Washington's birthday. History is the nation's memory. No history—no national memory—no identity."

Alexander Solzhenitsyn, the great Russian writer, received the Templeton Prize for Progress in Religion in 1993. In his speech, he spelled out the reason his country had fallen on hard times—they had forgotten God:

> More than half a century ago, when I was a child, I recall a number of older people offer the following explanation for the great disasters that had befallen Russia: Men have forgotten God; that's why all this has happened. Since then I have spent well-nigh 50

years working on the history of our revolution. In the process I have read hundreds of books, collected hundreds of personal testimonies, and have already contributed eight volumes of my own toward the effort of clearing away the rubble left by that upheaval. But if I were asked today to formulate as concisely as possible the main cause of the ruinous Russian revolution that swallowed up some 60 million of our people, I could not put it more accurately than to repeat, "Men have forgotten God; that's why all this has happened."

Five years earlier, Solzhenitsyn had spoken at Harvard University. In that 1978 speech, he said that America must return to God, at which point he was booed. He said that hurt him more deeply than his suffering in the Russian gulag. We would do well to remember the words of Deuteronomy 6:12, ". . . take care lest you forget the LORD. . ."

Is America at the crossroads or did we long ago pass that juncture, make some bad choices, and are we now heading in the wrong direction? Have we collided with an iceberg but don't know it? Are the waters even now rushing into the watertight compartments down below? If so, why does the dancing continue in the first-class ballroom?

2

The Unbreakable Covenant

Amerca's future is not guaranteed. Nations die. The landscape of history is cluttered with the rubble of civilizations that rose, flourished, lingered awhile, and disappeared. There are no guarantees, but some things are certain. One of those certainties is God's promise to bless those who bless Abraham. The promise comes with a warning: "And I will curse him who curses you." Neither promise nor warning have ever been abrogated; they apply to all people, for all time. The promise means resisting those voices calling for Israel's virtual surrender; and protesting the growing pressure coming from every quarter demanding concessions that would result, ultimately, in their elimination.

Dispatches from the daily press are a wake-up call: "Israel's survival could be in jeopardy unless it reaches a peace deal with the Palestinians." "Support of Israel to be balanced against other interests."

Our national sins are already piled high, and are grievous. To betray the Jewish people, to desert them in their growing isolation, could trigger a chain of events bringing this country to its knees.

The miracle is that this nation has survived at all. Its history stretches from the burning bush to the gas chambers, from the parting of the Red Sea to the death camps, from the glory of the first temple to the horror of the "final solution." History will not last long enough to erase the memory of the atrocities of the Holocaust, of the roads of Europe choked with fleeing Jews nobody wanted and no nation was prepared to welcome.

The last half of the twentieth century is indelibly stained with the shame and infamy of nations—including the United States and Britain—that sealed off escape routes and closed their borders to these children of Abraham.

"If you wait long enough, the historians assure us, the blows of time will eventually do their work on everyone," Prime Minister Benjamin Netanyahu writes. "But the Jews were a problem. They received more blows than any other nation, yet they refused to die." He cites Fredrick the Great, a skeptic, who once asked his chaplain, "Can you give me any good evidence that God exists?" The chaplain answered, "Yes, the Jews."

Addressing a joint session of the United States Congress, then-prime minister Shimon Peres described Israel as a small nation forty miles wide and four thousand years deep. "Nowhere in the world is there a country like the land of Israel," Peres noted, "where so many weapons and so many holy places occupy such a small area." Mark Train, who visited Palestine in 1869, was surprised by its size, "I suppose it was because I could not conceive of a small country having so large a history."

How small is it? We're talking about a little country on the eastern rim of the Mediterranean so small you can hardly find it on a map. Half the size of West Virginia, harboring fewer people than the state of Georgia, it has a landmass of 10 thousand square miles compared to five million square miles occupied by Arab states, a ratio of 540 to one.

This is the country, by the way, the European Union branded "the number one threat to world peace," whose occupants are assured that their future happiness and security lie in the ceding of yet another chunk of their national homeland to a neighbor sworn to their obliteration.

Searching the Scriptures and tracking the Jews throughout history, one is struck by their uniqueness. For one thing, they are a mere handful, as Moses declared, "The LORD did not set his love upon you nor choose you because you were more in number than any other people, for you were the least of all peoples" (Deut. 7:7). Their influence on every aspect of human life—finance, statecraft, art, medicine, music, education, science, is strikingly disproportionate to their size.

They are a people set apart. The centuries of dislocation, deprivation, imprisonment, the threat of assimilation—and the wandering years, which saw their character maligned, their synagogues burned, their cemeteries defaced, could not alter, but rather underscored the fact that they are marked. Try as they may, they cannot escape their chosenness.

In *Why the Jews? The Reason for Anti-Semitism*, Dennis Prager and Joseph Telushkin pose the question: Why? "Sooner or later, nearly every Jewish child, after a rejection, an insult, or a beating, asks himself the question. From the earliest Jewish history, through practically every era, in every country where they have lived, and some where they have not, there has been hatred of the Jews."

Golda Meir grew up in Milwaukee where she attended Fourth Street School, and loved it, but she knew she was different. "And, above all, I remember being aware that this was happening to me because I was Jewish, which made me different from most of the other children in the yard. It was a feeling that I was to know again many times during my life—the fear, the frustration, the consciousness of being different and the profound instinctive believe that if one wanted to survive, one had to take effective action about it personally."

Two and a half centuries ago, Jean-Jacques Rousseau put his finger on this uniqueness: "The Jews present us with an outstanding spectacle: the laws of Numa, Lycurgus, and of Solon are dead; the far more ancient ones of Moses are still alive. Athens and Sparta and Rome have perished and their people have vanished from the earth; though destroyed, Zion has not lost her children. They mingle with all the nations but are not lost among them; they no longer have their leaders, yet they are still a nation; they no longer have a country, and yet they are still citizens."

Byron lyricized Israel's centuries-long dilemma in Hebrew Melodies:

> *The wild dove hath her nest,*
> *the fox his cave;*
> *Mankind their country,*
> *Israel but the grave.*

The yearning to escape the grave was illustrated by the remarks of an Israeli cabinet minister. Pastors and rabbis had been invited to a luncheon in Memphis to meet with several Knesset members and their legal counsel to the United Nations. "We heard some country," said one of the ministers, referring to an event the night before in Nashville. "There was singing and dancing. We had forgotten what it was like to be happy. We long to be simply happy. We want to live to see our children go out to play without fear—to grow up and not have to join the army. We have brought water out of the desert, built universities, and developed one of the best armies in the world. One thing that we long for is to live in peace."

The long journey to a country of their own where their children could live without fear, where they could be "simply happy," began in earnest in the last two decades of the nineteenth century. A 36-year-old Paris correspondent for a Viennese newspaper, aroused by the growing anti-Semitism in Europe, took concrete measures to provide a refuge for victims of Russian massacres and mistreatment elsewhere. Theodor Herzl lived only eight more years, but in those brief years set in motion a movement called Zionism which would not end until May 14, 1948, when at four o'clock in the afternoon at Tel Aviv museum on Rothschild Boulevard, Prime Minister David Ben-Gurion, dressed in dark suit and tie, stood up, rapped the gavel, and said, "I shall now read the Scroll of Independence."

Golda Meir remembered, "It took only a quarter of an hour to read the entire proclamation. Then, as though a signal had been given, we rose to our feet, crying and clapping, while Ben-Gurion, his voice breaking for only the first time, read: "'The State of Israel will be open to Jewish immigration and the in gathering of exiles.'"

Like the bush in the wilderness that burned unconsumed, so Israel, hunted down, terrorized, imprisoned and murdered, refused to disappear. Rising from the ashes of Auschwitz, from the torture cells of Treblinka and Dachau, and staggering up out of the sewers of Warsaw, they returned to their historic homeland.

Now that they were a reborn nation, the question was how would they stay alive. By the morning of May 15, Israel was under armed attack from the north, the east, and the south. Egypt, Jordan, Lebanon, Syria, and Iraq concluded that the creation of an Israeli state was not a good idea and that it should be dismantled before the ink was dry on the paperwork.

By the time the fledgling nation had turned back the five

bully states, some things had been pretty well agreed upon. For starters, the Jews weren't going anywhere. Their collective memory was heavy with sights and sounds and smells and images too horrible to remember, too awful to forget, and they vowed never again to be driven from their homes to wander defenseless in hostile lands. They were certainly in no mood to be lectured by nations that had refused them the time of day when their lives were in jeopardy.

Golda Meir said she would have been much more nervous when she met with the Pope on January 16, 1973, had he not started the visit by "telling me that he found it hard to accept the fact the Jews—who, of all people, should have been capable of mercy toward others because they had suffered so terribly themselves—had behaved so harshly in their own country. Well, that is the kind of talk I can't bear, particularly since it is not true that we have mistreated the Arabs."

"Your Holiness," Meir addressed the Pope, "do you know what my own very earliest memory is? It is waiting for a pogrom in Kiev. Let me assure you that my people know all about real harshness, and also that we learned all about real mercy when we were being led to the gas chambers of the Nazis."

The years that followed were marked by intense effort and unrelenting struggle. Survival depended upon finding water where there was no water, turning swamps into gardens, building homes and schools and universities, not to mention forging a government and building a national defense.

There were wars and rumors of wars. Armies massed on the borders, saboteurs and suicide bombers breached the perimeters, and too often promised aid from friendly countries did not come. But the dream expressed by Shimon Peres became a conviction: "We can wash this blood-soaked land of conflict with living water, we can grow flowers on the battlefields of the past and bring smiles to Jewish and Arab children—indeed, to all our children, who will inherit our land and live there in happiness and peace."

The cost of cleansing that blood-soaked land over the last half century has come at a premium, but a promise had been made to the dead and the yet unborn, and that promise would be kept. The reborn nation geared up for instant mobilization. Former refugees and returning exiles became warriors. Public parks were converted to cemeteries where fallen warriors lie buried.

Israel's rebirth during the twentieth century was not an accident of history but a fulfillment of prophetic Scripture: "Here the word of the LORD, and declare it in the isles afar off, and say, 'He that scattered Israel will gather him and keep him as a shepherd does his flock'" (Jer. 31:10).

"He will set up a banner for the nations, and will assemble the outcasts of Israel and gather together the dispersed of Judea from the four corners of the earth" (Isa. 11:12).

"For I will take you from among the nations, and gather you out of all countries and bring you into your own land" (Ezek. 36:24).

This is the story of a people whose history reaches back four thousand years—and who are front-page news every morning. Try as they may, their enemies cannot destroy them.

At four o'clock on the morning of April 29, 1945, on what would be the last day of his life, Adolf Hiller dictated his political testament. His last words to the German people were, "Above all I charge the leaders of the nation and those under them to scrupulous observance of the laws of race and to merciless opposition to the universal poisoner of all peoples, International Jewry."

But Hitler didn't have the last word; He died that night by his own hand. His loyal staff burned and buried his body in the courtyard of his bunker. Today a sovereign Israeli state bursts its seams and finds its place—albeit tenuously—among the nations. And the Word of God is unaltered: "If you can break my covenant with the day and my covenant with the night, so that there will not be day and night in their season, then My covenant may also be broken with David My servant" (Jer. 33:20:21).

The purposes of God are not open to debate and He never reneges on a promise. The question facing the United States is, shall we in the face of mounting, global opposition and hostility toward Israel, "bless" these sons of Abraham, or shall we side with those who say, "Come, and let us cut them off from being a nation, that the name of Israel may be remembered no more"? (Ps. 83:4). Our survival as a nation may hinge on our answer to that question.

3

Why Johnny Can't Read

The education of the young was not an afterthought with the Puritans. Rearing children in the fear of the Lord was a sacred trust, a *parental* responsibility. The idea of a federal role was unimaginable and would not have been tolerated during the first two hundred years of our history. The voyagers who survived the long ocean journey took seriously what they had read in the only book they brought with them from the old country:

> And these words which I command you today shall be in your heart. You shall teach them diligently to your children, and shall talk of them when you sit in your house, and when you walk by the way, when you lie down, and when you rise up (Deut. 6:6, 7).

The mandate was clear and the philosophy of instruction simple. Education begins with answers, not questions. All ideas are not equal. When the training of children is reduced to searching for a truth that is either unknowable, or is no better than someone else's "truth," the whole enterprise becomes what someone has called a moral scavenger hunt, and "we ought not be surprised, when the hunt is over, at what some of the children have brought in."

There was no question as to the role of parents in teaching the young, nor was there confusion as to subject matter. These sons and daughters of Pilgrims were taught who God is, what God has done, and what God requires. If it were argued that such a curriculum is simplistic, or naïve, let it be noted that it produced George Washington, James Madison, Patrick Henry, Robert Sherman, Benjamin Rush, John Adams, George Mason and other intellectual giants who signed a declaration of independence, led a revolution, wrote a constitution, and bequeathed to succeeding generations a nation unlike any other in history.

The United States was the first country in the world to recognize the necessity of educating all of its citizens. Our forefathers believed every child should be able to read and write. During colonial times, less than four percent of the nation's children were illiterate, all of them home-schooled or educated in church- or charity-funded private schools that flourished—without support from the state. Poor children had scholarship money available from sponsors.

It was not unusual for colonial children to have read the entire Bible at an early age. Youngsters were ready for college at 13 and 14. It is not uncommon today to meet college students who can scarcely read a chapter in the Bible without faltering and who are unable to write a decent paragraph of English. Our fathers knew something we seem to have forgotten—the fear of the Lord is the beginning of wisdom. That's the starting point; beyond that was the pursuit of knowledge, exploring the wonder of God's creation beginning with the act of creation itself and tracing the handiwork of God in a thousand directions.

In a later chapter were listed four things Henry Steel Commager argues had altered the course of our history. The third one he cites should not be passed over with indifference; its significance is profound--education was no longer under the control of Protestant Christians. This set in motion a chain of events that has had far-reaching and devastating consequences.

It is important to understand how seriously early Americans took this business of preparing their children to face life. One of the first books printed in this country was *The New England Primer*. First published in 1690, it became the primary textbook in our schools and together with the Bible fashioned the character and formed the building blocks of a nation that would become the envy of the world. *The Primer* presented practical advice and Bible truths in rhythmic form for easy memorization. It contained the Westminster Catechism, prayers and hymns. In those days, one did not feel like a foreigner in his own country if he brought a Bible to school.

In addition to *The New England Primer*, over five million copies of Noah Webster's spelling book were purchased by private citizens. In a country of under 20 million people that was almost one per household.

In the 10 years between 1813 and 1823, Sir Walter Scott's novels sold five million copies—an amount equal to about 60 million books today. James Fenimore Cooper's books, including *The Last of the Mohicans*, also sold in the millions. These best sellers were not light reading. Pick up a copy of a Scott at your local library and you will discover complex, highly allusive prose that would challenge any college student today.

In 1812, Pierre DuPont de Nemours published *Education in the United States*, a book chronicling America's phenomenally high rate of literacy. "Forty years before passage of the compulsory school laws," DuPont noted, "fewer than four out of every thousand people in the new nation could not read and do numbers well."

DuPont was also amazed that nearly every child was skilled in "argumentation," the old-fashioned term for critical thinking. He attributed this to the widespread habit of involving young children in discussions about the meaning of difficult Bible passages.

So how are we doing today? Why do American presidents and many members of Congress, while promoting public education, send their own children to private institutions? Why are schools from the ghettos to the suburbs like a boiling cauldron? Why are some teachers in a constant state of fear? Why are armed guards necessary to protect students and teachers? Why can't Johnny read? Why do test scores for high school seniors stagnate while public spending skyrockets? The old one-room schools, even in unpromising backwoods environments, were capable of producing not only an Abraham Lincoln, but a literate population fully capable of following Lincoln-Douglas debates, some of which went on for two or three hours. The 1990 National Assessment of Educational Progress (NAEP) concluded that more than half of our elementary, middle, and high school students are unable to demonstrate competency in English, mathematics, science, history, and geography. Further, even fewer appear to be able to use their minds well.

More than a decade after *A Nation at Risk* drew attention to America's educational mediocrity, the reading proficiency of nine- and 13-year-olds has declined even further. Only three percent of American fourth, eighth, and twelfth graders can write above a "minimal" or "adequate" level, according to the 1992 Writing Report Card. The test, which rated students' writing abilities on a scale of one to six, found that fewer than one in 30 children earned a score high enough to indicate they write effectively or persuasively. That's only three percent.

Is this by design, or is something nefarious going on? A clue is found in the life and times of John Dewey, a towering influence in American life, whom we shall meet in a moment. Paul Blanchard in *The Humanists*, March/April 1976, makes it clear that the goal is to keep your children under their influence and away from you as parents as long as possible. Keep the kids in school until they are 16 or 17 and Adam and Eve won't stand a change. The kind of Bible-based Christianity that disembarked from the Mayflower must be expunged if the transformation of the country is to be complete.

"Never," writes author and education Samuel Blumenfeld, "have we had more reading experts, remedial specialists, and doctors of education devoted to reading. Never has more money been poured into reading 'research,' and never have we had more illiteracy affecting every level of society."

The seriousness of the situation was described by Karl Shapiro, the eminent poet-philosopher who taught for many years at the University of California. He told the California Library Association in 1970:

> What is really distressing is that this generation cannot and does not read. I am speaking of university students in what are supposed to be our best universities. Their illiteracy is staggering. . . . We are experiencing a literacy breakdown which is unlike anything I know of in the history of letters.

The problem of failing schools arises not from the incompetence and indifference of dedicated teachers, but from the policy makers, social planners, and union masters. Blumenfeld writes, "The National Education Association is probably the most intellectually dishonest organization in America." Why? Because it is more interested in acquiring power to advance its radical political and social ends than it is in teaching children to read and write and add two and two. And they make no bones about it. These are the people who advanced the idea that "teachers should seek power in order to transform America into a socialist society." Professor George S. Counts of Teachers College put it quite bluntly in his 1932 book, *Dare the School Build a New Social Order*. He said his firm conviction was "that the teachers should deliberately reach for power and then make the most of their conquest." And they put their money where their mouth is. In 2016, the NEA, the nation's largest union, gave $33.2 million in political contributions, 93 percent to liberal causes. This is not to suggest that there aren't many well-qualified teachers in our public schools who give it their best, sometimes under difficult circumstances, but they are caught up in a union designed by an ideological system inimical to the bedrock principles that made our country the envy of the world.

We are too soon forgetful of our history. There existed in early America a distinct relationship between the church, the Bible, and education that carried over into all aspects of life. During the first hundred years of the colonial period, 126 colleges had been established--all by a Christian group or church denomination. In 1840, the president of every major university in America was a clergyman or a person trained to work in the church. Less than twenty years after the Pilgrims landed at Plymouth Rock, the Reverend John Harvard was instrumental in founding a university where young men could be trained to preach the gospel. When Harvard University was founded in 1636, it was dedicated *In Chrisiti Gloriam*, "To the Glory of Christ." *Veritas*—the present motto came along seven years later at the suggestion of Henry Dunster, the first president of the university. *Veritas* was another way of recognizing Jesus Christ, who was seen as the ultimate Truth.

At the main entrance of Harvard University, visitors can still read John Harvard's original purpose in founding the institution. The inscription reads:

Let the main end of every student's life and studies be to know God and Jesus Christ which is eternal life. And therefore to lay Christ in the bottom as the only foundation of all sound knowledge and learning.

As late as 1796, the Harvard rule book stated, "If you doubt that the Scriptures are the Word of God, you are subject to immediate dismissal."

Before long, however, the educational elites who had studied abroad, brought back from universities and schools of theology in Germany a virulent strain of unbelief that undermined confidence in the Scriptures. Once that confidence had eroded, the deity of Jesus was soon rejected along with other foundational truths. By 1805, Harvard University which had for 169 years trained young men to preach the gospel, had become a citadel of secular humanist teaching.

The virus would spread and affect other institutions of learning. Fifty years after the takeover of Harvard, in 1861, Massachusetts Institute of Technology (MIT) became the first college chartered by atheists—only 72 years after the founding of our country.

In 1985 Ari Goldman took a leave from his job as religion reporter for the New York Times and enrolled in the Harvard Divinity School. To deepen his knowledge of the world's religions, the orthodox Jew spent a year studying Buddhism, Hinduism, the African religions, Islam and others. He was not prepared for what he found when he came to the class on orthodox Christianity, he writes in *The Search for God at Harvard*. Everyone seemed embarrassed by the subject.

When a girl referred to John 11, where Jesus raises Lazarus from the dead, there were audible snickers in the room. Noon worship, "would include some tepid hymns, an inoffensive reading from Scripture and a short sermon, usually on the liberal political topic of the day. Occasionally," he said, "I would see someone sitting there meditating, but in my entire year at Harvard, I never saw anyone on his or her knees."

If the divinity of Jesus was mentioned, the teacher would offer an apology to the non-Christian in the room. A Christian prayer at convocation would be followed by a Buddhist meditation for balance. "Religious truth did not seem to exist at the divinity school," Goldman commented, "only relativism." One wonders what Jesus did to deserve such a bad reputation?

A student can graduate from this historic institution of learning without ever coming to grips with the central questions of life: What is its meaning, why are we here, how did it all start? Writing in *Harvard's Crisis of Faith* in *Newseek.com*, Lisa Miller says, "To dismiss the importance of the study of faith—especially now—out of academic narrow-mindedness is less than unhelpful. It is unreasonable."

That's the story of the first university in the United States, founded for the express purpose of training young men for Christian ministry. And it illustrates how departure from a belief in biblical authority opens the floodgates of unbelief affecting religion, politics, government and business—and, ultimately the future of the country.

By 1795, Yale University's student body was suffering from the same malady that had decimated Harvard. Lyman Beecher, an undergraduate at the time, wrote, "The college was in a most ungodly state. The college church was almost extinct. Most of the students were skeptical and rowdies were plenty."

In an effort to restore Christian principles, the administration appointed Dr. Timothy Dwight, a committed Christian, as president of the school. He immediately fired every faculty member who was not committed to the Word of God. Then the new president, grandson of theologian Jonathan Edwards, invited the students to chapel and said something like this: "You tell me why you don't accept the Bible, why you believe what you do, and why you live like you do. Take as long as you wish, with the proviso that when you are finished, you will listen to me."

The students agreed. They defended their careless lifestyle, giving the new president their reasons for believing that God is irrelevant, that the Bible is not to be taken seriously. When they had finished, Timothy Dwight brilliantly and with passion shattered their complacency, overturned their arguments—and got their attention:

> There can be no halting between two opinions. You must meet face to face the bands of disorder, of falsehood and of sin. What part hath he that belie-veth with an infidel? . . . Will you imbibe their prin-ciples? Will you teach your children that death is an eternal sleep, and that the end sanctifies the means, that moral obligation is a dream, religion a farce? Will you become the rulers of Sodom and the people of Gomorrah? Will you enthrone the goddess of rea-son before the tale of Christ? Will you burn your Bi-bles? Will you crucify anew your Redeemer? Will you deny your God?

Dwight talked about the joy of fulfillment that comes from laboring with Christ and the strength needed to choose the right in the light of eternity:

> The most important consideration is yet to be sug-gested. A consideration infinitely awful and glori-ous, there may be a hereafter! The course of sin be-gun here may continue forever. The seed of virtue sown in the present world and raised to a young and feeble item may be destined to grow immortal.

Dr. H. Humphrey, who later became the president of Amherst College, was an undergraduate at Yale at that time, describes the impact of President Dwight's preaching on the students:

It came with power as had never been witnessed within these walls before. It was in the freshman year of my own class. It was like a mighty, rushing wind. The whole college was shaken. It seemed for a long time as if the whole mass of students would press into the kingdom. It put a new faith on the college.

Many students came to salvation during the years of revival at Yale. Benjamin Silliman, who later became a chemistry teacher at Yale, wrote to his mother about the effects of the revival: "Yale College has become a little temple. Prayer and praise seem to be the delight of the greater part of the students while those who are still unfeeling are awed into respectful silence."

The result was a spiritual awakening that not only shook the college but touched the nation. Bernard A. Weisberger, in his book, *They Gathered at the River*, describes it this way: "Since Yale was transforming much of the intellectual leadership of New England, not to say the whole country, this was a fact of transcendent importance in American history."

Dozens of young men were saved and called into the ministry, among them Lyman Beecher. His eldest daughter, Harriet Beecher Stowe, later wrote *Uncle Tom's Cabin*, which played a part in the abolition of slavery; illustrating the connection between church and culture and demonstrating how the great social breakthroughs in the world have come directly or indirectly from the church, all of them.

The epic and unyielding battle for truth starts with the children. I traced the origin of that battle on a recent visit to Boston. I walked up Tremont Avenue one afternoon to the old Park Street Church; visited a cemetery nearby where headstones bear the names of revered forefathers; then walked another block to the Massachusetts State House which sits proudly across the street from the oldest park in America, the Boston Common.

Touring the magnificent capitol building with its impressive rotunda and marble hallways, I admired the pictures and framed speeches, the tapestries, statues, and memorabilia. On my way out, a sculpture caught my eye. Perched on a pedestal by a side door, it depicted two hands holding the world. A bronze marker identified the artfully crafted object simply, *Creation.*

I stepped outside to be greeted by a larger-than-life statue of the father of public education in America, Horace Mann, and was reminded of the age-long battle between God the Creator and man the creature; the creature would usurp the place of God and, employing children as pawns, create his own world without divine intervention.

The pieces of the puzzle came together as I walked another block and discovered the headquarters of the Unitarian Church. That was of great interest to me knowing that Mann was a Unitarian. A brochure in the lobby outlines the tenants of faith:

> Unitarian Universalism has differed from mainline Western and Eastern faiths by claiming that truth is multifaceted and elusive. Whereas there may be many different truths in our lives, The Truth is not accessible to human grasp.

Unitarian-Universalist minister Greta Crosby declares, "I want to tell the truth, the whole truth and nothing but the truth, but The Truth is not simple but complex." The brochure further states, "You will find no single pathway to God or enlightenment, instead there are numerous worthy routes that have been demonstrated by Unitarian-Universalists throughout history."

On May 5, 1819, William Ellery Channing delivered "The Baltimore Sermon" in which he claimed reason rather than revelation as the instrumental source of his faith. That sermon, in effect, launched the Unitarian controversy and denomination. As we have seen, the results were far-reaching. When unbelief flourishes in the pulpit it taints everything it touches. Such was the case in 1819.

Unitarians reject the Bible as the inspired Word of God, the deity of Jesus, and the doctrine of the Trinity. "Furthermore, we come to our religious values experientially. The beliefs we hold are not so much revealed to us as experienced by us."

With that statement in mind, it is not hard to understand their philosophy of education: "We encourage our children to develop their own working wisdoms instead of inheriting the truths of their parents or tradition."

Unlike the earlier colonists who considered it their divine mandate to pass on the truths of God's Word to their children, the Unitarians encourage their offspring to make up their own version of wisdom and truth.

Having abandoned the church, the secular humanists needed a platform for their new religion. As intellectuals who worshiped the mind of man, it was natural for them to use the medium of public education as their stage.

An atheist by the name of Robert Owen founded the "friends of education," a group made up of socialists, Freethinkers, Unitarians, Universalists and others. According to Samuel Blumenfeld in *Is Public Education Necessary*, these men set out to change the way we train our youth by employing the model of European education.

As early as 1830 they established three principles which remain the framework for public education to this day: Make school attendance compulsory, establish government-sponsored "free" schools, and form teacher training schools they control in order to prepare the teacher of the future.

These friends of education succeeded in having the Massachusetts Legislature establish the nation's first state board of education. The group hired Horace Mann as its secretary in 1836, and the secularization of Massachusetts' schools was underway. Mann went on to become the first United States secretary of education, and with an agenda based on the rejection of orthodox

Christianity sought to destroy its influence in American public life, as Richard Baer explains:

> Horace Mann and other proponents of public education were intent on reforming society by changing the values of children. Mann had little sympathy for Calvinism or Catholics, and he was determined to use every legal means—including state coercion in schooling—to ensure that other people's children were taught the truth as he understood it.

This hostility reflected his faith in the new religion which claimed that nothing is absolute, nothing is fixed, and that man's ideas are superior to divine revelation. This is the basis of many current public school textbooks and reflects the mindset of many educators, whose approach is: Truth is not something to be found once and for all, but is forever in the making. All ideas are equal.

Knowing he could not "improve" society through legislation or working through adults, Horace Mann hit on an idea: aim for the children. In 1837, he wrote a friend to explain his strategy:

> I have abandoned jurisprudence, and betaken myself to the larger sphere of mind and morals, having found the present generation composed of materials almost unmalleable, I'm about transferring my efforts to the next generation. Men are cast iron but children are wax.

Mann saw public schools as a vehicle for state control. A PBS television segment on homeschooling removes any ambiguity as to how the social planners view the role of parents in child development. Professor Robert Reich of Stanford University worries that the state might find itself shortchanged in its "interest in knowing that children are growing up to become well-rounded citizens."

> If parents can control every aspect of a kid's education, shield them from exposure to the things that the parents deem sinful or objectionable, screen in only the things which accord to their convictions—and not allow them exposure to the world of a democracy—will the children grow up then basically in the image of their own parents' beliefs?

The professor shows how generous and liberal-minded he is by adding, "I'm not anti-homeschooling in the sense that I want to see homeschooling banned, I just want good regulations to apply to those parents who choose to homeschool."

Without some kind of regulation, the professor fears, the state won't know what's going on in our homes, what mom and dad are teaching the kids. This is the mindset of people like Harvard education Charles M. Pierce, who in a 1972 keynote address to a teachers' group warned:

> Every child in America at the age of five is mentally ill because he comes to school with certain allegiances toward our founding fathers, toward our elected officials, toward his parents, toward a belief in a supernatural being and it's up to you teachers to make all of these sick children well.

The militant goal of the secularists is summarized in an award-winning essay by John Dunphy in the *American Humanist Association* in 1983:

> The battle for humankind's future must be waged and won in the public school classroom by teachers who correctly perceive their role as the proselytizers of a new faith, a religion of humanity. . . . These teach-

ers must embody the same selfless dedication as the most rabid fundamentalist preachers, for they will be ministers of another sort, utilizing classroom instead of a pulpit to convey humanist values in whatever subject they teach. The classroom must and will become an arena of conflict between the old and the new—the rotting corpse of Christianity, together with all its adjacent evils and misery, and the new faith of humanism, resplendent in its promise of a world in which the never-realized Christian ideal of "love by neighbor" is finally achieved.

If Horace Mann was the statist, John Dewey was the socialist, both of whom strove mightily to transform the country; and both saw the classroom as the vehicle through which change would come. Born in 1859 in Burlington, Vermont, Dewey was raised in a Christian family and taught Sunday School as a young man. Somewhere along the way he lost his faith, rejected theism and embraced the philosophy of pragmatism. Dewey was a prototype of the twenty-first century secularist. A thorough-going naturalist, he viewed humans only in their capacity as biological organisms. Bold and defiant in his atheism, he declared,

> Faith in the prayer-hearing God is an unproved and outmoded faith. There is no God and there is no soul. Hence, there are no needs for the props of traditional religion. With dogma and creed excluded, then immutable truth is also dead and buried. There is no room for fixed, natural law or moral absolutes.

Having abandoned the Bible, Dewey would devote the rest of his life to teaching, writing books and preparing curriculum from a perspective of naturalistic theory. No other single individual would leave such a big mark on America's public schools. And literacy was certainly not a priority, for people who read too well or too early are dangerous because they know how to find out what they don't know on their own without consulting experts. In an effort to eliminate people who could read "too well or too early," he advocated abandoning the phonics method of reading. Why? Because students who learned to read phonetically were able to master any word by sounding it out. With the "look-say" method, which Dewey espoused, students learned to read only those words taught them by their instructors. The ability to read challenging, mind-expanding material produces thinkers who can't easily be "socialized" or controlled, and that's the last thing humanist educators wanted. No independent, self-reliant thinkers need apply in this brave new world.

Leave God out of the equation and dumb down the children and you reap the whirlwind. The decline in America's literacy was not the result of an honest mistake made by good people but was actually programmed by social engineers. To think deeply, one must read deeply; and to be able to read deeply with proficiency was not encouraged by the social planners who knew better than the old Puritans with their Geneva Bible and *New England Primer*. And now you know why Johnny can't read, and what the implications of that might be.

Poor Adolf, if he only knew how often his name is invoked in the tumultuous and uncivil discourse of our time. He would turn over in his grave, wherever that is, if he knew how often he is blamed for much that goes wrong in our world. But the little Austrian colonial might be able to teach us something. Listen to the words of one of the most effective revolutionaries of all time: "When an opponent declares, 'I will not come over to your side,' I calmly say, 'Your child belongs to us already. What are you? You will pass on. Your descendants, however, now stand in the new camp. In a short time they will know nothing else but this new community.'" The date was 1939, the speaker Adolf Hitler, who accomplished the radical transformation of Germany virtually overnight by controlling the children. That kind of thing would not happen in this new land, not if the Puritans had anything to do with it. That's why to them the education of the young was a sacred trust. To be unfaithful to that trust is to signal the end of the American dream.

4

Truth or Consequences

Does it matter, really, what a man thinks, what he "practically lays to heart, and knows for certain?" Richard M. Weaver thought so. The English professor at the University of Chicago wrote a book in 1948 entitled *Ideas Have Consequences.*

The catastrophes of our age are not the product of necessity, but of intelligent choice, he argues. Failure to understand that ideas are consequential is a form of insanity. "There is ground for declaring that modern man has become a moral idiot," Weaver writes.

Does it matter, really, what a nation thinks? Is it not a form of insanity for a nation to blithely proceed on the skewed assumption that one can sow to the flesh and not reap corruption? Is history not witness to the wrecks of nations that have risen gloriously, sinned grievously, and died tragically? Let's examine a chapter out of history that demonstrates the truth that ideas have consequences.

Charles Darwin wrote a book in 1859 that changed the world. You can draw a straight line from the comfortable English home where the scientist put forth his views on the origin of human life, to the jaded philosophy of Friedrich Nietzsche, the twisted gospel of Karl Marx, Hitler's death camps, Stalin's gulag, the Killing Fields of Cambodia. If it seems unfair to lay so heavy a burden on the doorstep of one man, the record speaks for itself. Herbert Spencer read Darwin and boiled it down to a single phrase, "survival of the fittest." Hitler took that single phrase, and the philosophy behind it, and presided over the funeral of Germany. He transformed Europe's richest, best educated, and most cultured nation into a holocaust that haunts us to this day. The retarded, the schizophrenic, epileptics and deaf mutes, were put to death. It was called mercy killing. Get rid of war amputees, children with minor defects, even normal children with learning problems.

More than seven decades have passed into history since the Third Reich ceased to exist, but the passage of time has done little to resolve the questions surrounding the dark days of the rise and fall of the National Socialist German Workers' Party. How could one of the chief centers of civilized society have become a torture chamber for millions? How could a country proud of its schools and universities, its thinkers and its poets, produce a generation of monsters, fanatically anti-Semitic, brutal, profane and cruel beyond words? How did educated, well-intentioned, principled people overlook the savagery of the brawling SS thugs who roamed the streets spreading terror? How do you make the leap from classroom, lecture hall, and museum to torture cellars and death camps. Why was there no grassroots uprising when neighbors disappeared in the night, rumors of Gestapo "interrogation" abounded, and brute force was substituted for the rule of law? Notwithstanding the cunning and Machiavellian chicanery of the Nazis, it must never be forgotten that Adolf Hitler came to power legally. The people let it happen.

The majority of Germans in the 1930s were civil, religious, good folks; but they chose to turn a blind eye to the secret police, slave labor camps, and the rants of Aryan supremacy and anti-Semitism. Of the fifteen representatives of the various ministries gathered at the Berlin suburb of Wannsee on January 20, 1942, to clear up the fundamental problems of the "final solution," eight had doctorates from Berlin universities.

A rationale for the madness, this festering anti-Jewish animus, were one to be found, will not bring back the dead or console the living, but civilized human beings will go on searching for answers. How did this happen, and why? The magnitude of the brutality and horror seems almost irrational, but it will help to remember that ideas have consequences. A confluence of currents flowing through history, percolating, gathering force, burst into a gusher of terror in the third decade of the last century. Examining those currents and understanding their origin, and why they persisted, though not lessening the pain of the survivors, may prevent recurrence the world can ill afford.

Germany's defeat on the battlefield of WWI had stoked feelings of humiliation, bitterness and rage. The seeds of another world war lay dormant in the terms of the peace treaty of Versailles, but the seeds would not lie dormant for long. There were scores to be settled, blame assigned, losses recovered, and an empire regained. Not unaware of the unrest of the masses, an Austrian would-be artist, a dreamer, wandering the streets of Vienna like a vagabond, saw himself as the one to bring about the restoration. He would be Nietzsche's Superman. The failed beer hall putsch and a stint in prison would be followed by rallies, speeches, organizational meetings and some delays, but the passion never died.

Central to that passion was a fanatical anti-Semitism. As early as 1922, Hitler told Major Josef Hill: "Once I am really in power, my first and foremost task will be the annihilation of the Jews. As soon as I have the power to do so, I will have gallows built in rows at the *Marienplatz* in Munich, for example—as many as traffic allows. Then the Jews will be hanged indiscriminately, and they will remain hanging until they stink; they will hang there as long as the principles of hygiene permit. As soon as they have been untied, the next batch will be strung up, and so on down the line, until the last Jew in Munich has been exterminated. Other cities will follow suit, precisely in this fashion, until all Germany has been completely cleansed of Jews."

Anti-Semitism became an integral part of Nazi life. The Jews were the cause of every misfortune. "We Germans did not lose the war," was the mantra of the twenties, "it was the Jews who betrayed us." The course of action to be pursued was not debatable: "ruthless battle against them holds the key to national if not international survival."

Although anti-Semitism had existed in Germany and other European countries for hundreds of years, it was the racial component that lent new momentum to the hatred of Jews that in the words of Joseph Trachtenberg was "so vast and abysmal, so intense, that it leaves one gasping for comprehension."

For the first time in history, racial anti-Semitism was adopted as a policy by a major political party. "According to the Nazis," William Shirer writes in *The Rise and Fall of the Third Reich*, "the German people constituted the highest stratum of the Nordic-Aryan race, while the Jews were a sub-human race who perpetually undermined the sound structure of world affairs and sought to usurp the authority and leadership of the superior race."

From which corner of hell did such vulgar notions arise? What fed this rage? What explains the behavior of the Nazis that leaves the civilized world baffled after all these years? Ideas do have consequences, and of the men whose views had a profound impact on Hitler, three stand out. There was the memory and magic of the composer Richard Wagner with its appeal to nationalism and not-so-subtle racism. Amy Fay, an American pianist who once observed him in Berlin, writes, "When he conducts, he is almost beside himself with excitement. The orchestra catches his frenzy, and each man plays under a sudden inspiration. Every sinew in his body speaks, his whole appearance is of arrogance and despotism personified." Wagner's music evoked similar emotions at the Bayreuth festivals. The performance of his music, together with Hitler's mesmerizing oratory, enthralled the masses and heightened the sense of mission: the elimination of undesirable elements in the population and exaltation of the superior race in the expanding German hegemony.

Houston Steward Chamberlain, an Englishman by birth, was attracted to Germanic culture and eventually became a citizen of Germany. "His contribution to Nazism," according to professor Richard Terrell, "was two-fold. First, he worked out a purely racial conception of history, in which the Germans were seen as superior and specially gifted. Secondly, he separated the concept of 'Christ' from its biblical and historical foundations and in the process transformed Christ into a Teutonic hero."

Chamberlain, Wagner's son-in-law, with his strange and fantastic theories, fit neatly into the web of Hitler's demented worldview. Hitler revered the memory of Richard Wagner who died in 1883. He visited Chamberlain in 1927 when he lay dying and later attended his funeral.

Add the name Friedrich Wilhelm Nietzsche to the triumvirate and you have a glimpse into the mind of Adolf Hitler and some of the influences that shaped his thinking. It was Nietzsche who proclaimed the death of God. He wrote, "Do we not hear anything yet of the noise of the grave diggers who are burying God? Do we not smell anything yet of God's decomposition? Gods, too, decompose. God is dead and we killed him."

Nietzsche, son of a Lutheran minister who died in 1900, having disposed of God, suggested that a successor must be found.

In Nietzsche, a man becomes his own lawgiver and source of morality. He employs the concept of the "Superman" to express this autonomy. Writing of Nietzsche in the midst of World War II, Erich Kahler referred to him as "the man who started this revolution that threatens the foundations of the world."

These were Hitler's guiding stars. The views they espoused became the mainspring of the Holocaust: There is no transcendent deity; man is a brute, the world is a jungle, and individual lives are irrelevant and replaceable; cold and calculated brutality are substituted for compassion and sympathy; anti-Jewish sentiment is embraced and elevated with religious fervor; and because the masses are sheep for the slaughter, a man, a single man must rise. Hitler made his position crystal clear as to who that man should be when he wrote in the second volume of *Mein Kamph*: "I know exactly where I am going and nothing is going to prevent me getting there."

Now that the Nazi philosophy had been defined, its foundation laid, its program delineated, its leader chosen (by himself), Hitler's express was leaving the station. Nothing could stop it now but an aroused and vocal opposition. Unfortunately, from the earliest days of the rumblings and rumors of revolution, when Hitler's beer hall rants were being applauded by self-serving miscreants and lowlifes, the opposition, if not absent, was scarcely heard. Herein lies the explanation of the paradox of the Third Reich. "It was a system founded on terror, unworkable without the secret police and concentration camps; but it was also a system which represented the deepest wishes of the German people."

The life and career of Albert Speer is a microcosm of the nation. Speer was born into an upper middle class family in Mannheim on March 19, 1905. He would follow the example of his father and grandfather and pursue a career in architecture. His talent and background brought him to the attention of the Nazi leadership and before his thirtieth birthday he had risen to become Hitler's primary architect.

A highly educated intellectual with a pleasant personality, Speer was drawn into Hitler's inner circle and became one of the Fuehrer's few friends. He designed many of the buildings of the Third Reich and later became minister of armaments, responsible for providing war material. He was a brilliant man, and likeable, but a tragic manifestation of the German willingness to turn a blind eye to the barbarities committed by the Nazi party or the state, although as he would later write from Spandau prison, "the broken panes of Jewish shops vandalized during the Kristallnacht lay shattered in front of him."

The Nuremberg Trials found Speer guilty of war crimes and he was sentenced to 20 years in prison where he wrote his autobiography, *Inside the Third Reich.* "I shall never forget the account of a Jewish family going to their deaths," he wrote. "The husband with his wife and children on their way to die are before my eyes to this day."

He claims Hitler's magnetic force had reached out to him and taken hold of him before he knew what was happening. As a result, he says, "My inclination to be relieved of having to think, particularly about the unpleasant facts, helped to sway the balance."

He admits that by entering Hitler's party he had already, in essence, assumed responsibility that led to the brutalities of slave labor, "the destruction of war, and to the deaths of those millions of so-called undesirable stock—to the crushing of justice and the elevation of every evil."

Speer, who dined at Hitler's dinner table and enjoyed the perks of insider status, was too busy with a satisfying career to care that "somewhere, unnoticed, the party machinery was relentlessly settling accounts with the opponents of years of political struggles, and hundreds of thousands of people were trembling because of their descent, their religion, or their convictions."

Years later in Spandau, Speer read Ernst Cassirer's comment

on the men who of their own accord threw away man's highest privilege: to be an autonomous person. In *The Myth of the State*, Cassirer writes, "But here are men, men of education and intelligence, honest and upright men who suddenly give up the highest human privilege. They have ceased to be free and personal agents." And earlier, "Man no longer questions his environment; he accepts it as a matter course,"

One day in the summer of 1944, Speer's friend Karl Hanke, the Gauleiter of Lower Silesia, came to see him. In earlier times they had discussed the Polish and French campaigns, had spoken of the dead and wounded, the pain and agonies. "This time, sitting in the green leather easy chair in my office, he seemed confused and spoke falteringly with many breaks." Hanke insisted that Speer never accept an invitation to inspect a concentration camp in Upper Silesia. "Never, under any circumstances." Speer said that Hanke had seen something there which he was not permitted to describe and moreover could not describe.

"I did not query him, I did not query Himmler, I did not query Hitler," Speer confessed. "I did not speak with personal friends. I did not investigate—for I did not want to know what was happening there. Hanke must have been speaking of Auschwitz."

Writing in a prison cell where he had 20 years to think and to remember, Albert Speer said, "I was inescapably contaminated morally; from fear of discovering something which might have made me turn from my course, I had closed my eyes."

This is the story of one man, a good man, who started out drafting and executing buildings, who fell under Hitler's spell, and of his own accord threw away man's highest privilege. But it is more than the account of a single individual who sold his soul to the devil. It is a metaphor of a great people who, when they might have risen to oppose an enormous evil, succumbed to a subtle self-interest; *If this evil man will restore our honor, rebuild our economy and deal with these pesky Jews, we will overlook the not-so-nice methods he chooses to employ.*

Therein lay a tragedy that is beyond description, that leaves us "gasping for comprehension." Ideas have consequences. When the ideas are radical, violent and inexorably evil, one shouldn't be surprised if the consequences are apocalyptic.

5

Broken Cisterns

Human beings are stranger than fiction. God chides His people for their fickleness: "For My people have committed
two evils; they have forsaken Me, the fountain of living waters,
and hewn out cisterns—broken cisterns that can hold no water"
(Jeremiah 2:13).

It's like a man walking away from a faithful wife and em-
bracing second-hand merchandise, something of lesser quality.

The premise of this chapter is straightforward: Conform to
the concepts found in Old and New Testaments and enjoy the
benefits of liberty, or neglect and discard them and continue to
slide toward tyranny. The principle applies to individuals, to
churches, to nations.

In a 1768 election day sermon in Mansfield, Connecticut, the Reverend Richard Salter said, "God does not give men up to be slaves until they lose their national virtue and abandon themselves to slavery." It's as simple as that. A nation that is not tethered to a transcendent God will find itself chained to a merciless secularism. Where the Spirit of the Lord is, there is liberty. Where He is absent, freedom is stifled and disappears.

That's why this irrational clamor for "change" is so unsettling. It's almost a fetish. On October 30, 2008, then-senator Barrack Obama told a large crowd of cheering supports, "We are five days away from fundamentally changing the United States of America." A former vice president calls for a "wrenching transformation of society" and a change of "the very foundation of our civilization."

Really? What's wrong with our foundation? Why does it need transforming, who is to determine how that transformation shall be accomplished, and how will we know when the makeover is complete? A more ominous question: Will we even recognize the place once the change agents are done? Men pledged their lives, their fortunes and their sacred honor to lay the foundation of this republic; and the edifice built upon it came with a high price tag. Attempts by twenty-first century men to remake this country are like children enhancing a Rembrandt with water colors. Besides, foundations don't require periodic sprucing up; new doors and windows, maybe a paint job, but leave the foundation intact.

We're paying a heavy price for this penchant for change. "Every ingredient of the American identity is in the process of being permanently replaced," writes Balint Vazsonyi. "Change has become a 'good' word. Change is good because 'nothing should go on forever' . . . We are abandoning our recipe for a successful society because we have been persuaded that all proposed changes will be for the better."

Vazsonyi writes from a unique perspective. He survived Nazi

conquest and escaped communist rule in his native Hungary. He became a naturalized citizen of the United States and never got over the wonder of it, the richness of his adopted home. Nor could he understand why his fellow citizens could so recklessly throw it all away. "What has happened to our common sense," he asks, "that could make us believe we can change all the ingredients and still retain the original article?"

This irrational clamor for change is troubling, but it is terrifying to learn that its proponents are not irrational. The proposals they advance for the radical altering of our society did not appear out of thin air. They were designed with purpose and care. They are pieces of a plan, clearly spelled out, the script deliberate and stark. The seeds of this alteration of our way of life were planted long ago, but the fruit sprang up in the 1960s. Since those days, men and women who seem to despise their own country have been pleading for a world stripped of the old Christian morality. They are dissatisfied with what we have and determined to change it.

It is unsettling that some among us do not treasure the gift of our national heritage. They will stop at nothing—including deceit and lies—to achieve their ends, using the power of persuasion when possible, the persuasion of power when necessary. It is doubly tragic that too many Americans are unmindful of the threat.

It was another time, another place, another people clamoring for change. Bored with "fountains of living water," they lusted for broken cisterns that hold no water. We want a king, they demanded; we want to be like other nations.

Have it your way; you shall have a king—but let me describe his behavior:

This will be the behavior of the king who will reign over you: He will *take* your sons and appoint them for his own chariots and to be his horsemen, and some of them will run before his chariots. He will appoint captains over his thousands and captains over his fifties, will set some to plow his ground and reap his harvest, and some to make His weapons of war and equipment for his chariots. He will *take* your daughters to be perfumers, cooks, and bakers. And he will *take* the best of your fields, your vineyards, and your olive groves, and give them to your servants. He will *take* a tenth of your grain and your vintage and give it to his officers and servants. And he will *take* your male servants, your female servants, your finest young men, and your donkeys, and put them to his work. He will *take* a tenth of your sheep. And you will be his servants. And you will cry out in that day . . ." (1 Sam. 8:11-18).

Read those verses again and count the number of times the word "take" occurs. Because of the tendency of government to take—your sons, your daughters, your property, your freedom—it was the intent of the authors of the Constitution to forge a document limiting the long reach of that government. It was the overriding concern of the men who went to Philadelphia in 1787. Our forefathers, having fled tyranny, recognized the danger inherent in any kind of authority, warned against its abuse, and incorporated safeguards in the Constitution to protect the people from that abuse.

It is the impulse of government to take; it's like an addiction. Because it has no money of its own, it takes yours. It confiscates private property to fulfill public promises. To satisfy the needs of the neighbors, it dips into the assets of the neighborhood.

Our ancestors did not come to the new world on a lark. The Mayflower voyage was no laughing matter. Its occupants knew firsthand that absolute power corrupts absolutely and determined to form a government in which the rulers governed with the consent of the governed, a concept all but forgotten.

We have become pawns of politicians and bureaucrats, some of whom have long since abandoned the principles of the Founders. "The power to tax involves the power to destroy," said Supreme Court Justice Jim Marshall. The idea of assessing citizens for the privilege of living in their own country was put forward in 1841 in Great Britain—although tyrants and kings and caesars had been docking the people for centuries. John Maynard Keynes, the liberal British economist, espoused the idea of government control of economic policy, even if it required the confiscation of private wealth for the public interest. These policies, not only ruinous but dishonest, weakened the British Empire and became the principle influence of monetary policy in the United States.

What does that mean? That we look to Washington for security, for meaning. It's called statism, the state becomes a fact of life, almost a god. "The state becomes the reason for us to live," theologian R.C. Sproul says. "The state unifies, transcends, becomes absolute, and is eternal."

We recognize the legitimacy and necessity of constituted authority. In Romans chapter 13, in what some have called the most important document in the political history of Western civilization, the Bible is clear on the subject:

> Let every soul be subject to the governing authorities. For there is no authority except from God, and the authorities that exist are appointed by God. Therefore whoever resists the authority resists the ordinance of God, and those who resist will bring judgment on themselves. For rulers are not a terror to good works, bit to evil. Do you want to be unafraid of the authority? Do what is good, and you will have praise from the same. For he is God's minister to you for good. But if you do evil, be afraid; for he does not bear the sword in vain; for he is God's minister, an avenger to

execute wrath on him who practices evil. Therefore you must be subject, not only because of wrath but also for conscience sake. For because of this you also pay taxes, for they are God's ministers attending continually to this very thing. Render therefore to all their due: taxes to whom taxes are due, customs to whom customs, fear to whom fear, honor to whom honor (Romans 13:1-7).

The levying of taxes is a necessary and useful function of government. When done judiciously by competent and responsible authorities, it is appropriate. But we have long passed that point, and have embraced practices that are obscene. Our excessive spending and dishonest taxation would have embarrassed the men who came before us, and threaten the economic survival of the country our children will inherit.

In a speech to the National Conference Board in 1943, Henning Webb Prentis, Jr., President of the Armstrong Cork Company, had this to say:

Again and again after freedom has brought opportunity and some degree of plenty, the competent become selfish, luxury-loving and complacent. The incompetent and the unfortunate grow envious, and covetous, and all three groups turn aside from the hard road of freedom to worship the Golden Calf of economic security. The historical cycle seems to be: From bondage to spiritual faith; from spiritual faith to courage; from courage to liberty; from liberty to abundance; from abundance to selfishness; from selfishness to apathy; from apathy to dependency; and from dependency back to bondage once more.

It is not difficult to conclude that America is well on its way through the cycle. Are we living in the twilight of a great civilization, or do we have the ability to recognize our plight and make necessary corrections?

It is impossible to make an objective assessment of the future without undertaking a realistic assessment of the past. It is necessary to examine our roots and trace our lineage if we are to understand where we are in the great scheme of things. In an earlier chapter we tracked the movement of the colonists from Cape Cod to Philadelphia and beyond. With some pride and much gratitude we rehearsed the steps taken to lay a foundation and raise the superstructure of a place called the United States of America.

For those who have been too busy to notice, or who may not care, we jumped the tracks four or five decades ago, and, racing wildly, are veering off in an uncertain direction, not sure who is at the controls. We seem to have lost our moorings. We're not certain about anything anymore. There is no true north, no Bureau of Standards; your guess is as good as mine.

This *laissez-faire* attitude toward truth, toward certitude, goes back roughly a hundred and fifty years to Charles Darwin. There were other voices before and after, but his book *The Origin of Species*, as we have noted, changed the world. It initiated a revolution in the history of thought that, for many, rendered God unnecessary, if not undesirable. The old beacons of the past were ignored. According to John Dewey, the great importance of *Origin* was in "laying hands upon the sacred ark of absolutely permanency."

In a similar vein, Sidney Ratner, one of Darwin's admirers, writes that "the most significant effect of Darwin's discovery was, not the triumph of certain specific scientific theories, but a revolutionary change in the very process by which men arrived at their convictions."

Those dying then knew where they went,
they went to God's right hand.

~ 62 ~

That hand is amputated now
and God cannot be found.
-Emily Dickinson

"A situation such as we seem to find ourselves in does, of course, entail the willingness to live more or less permanently in a state of uncertainty," writes Cynthia Eagle Russell in *Darwin in America*. "If science cannot offer us metaphysical certainty, then certainty is nowhere to be found (except, perhaps, for believers, in religion). But uncertainty seems in any case to be the lot of modern man. Few are the institutions of modern life which instill a sense of permanence; transience appears everywhere ascendant."

Ideas have consequences, and roots, ultimately, produce fruit. The gardens planted and cultivated by men who found God to be irrelevant have produced a bitter harvest that portends trouble down the road, the kind of trouble one finds when the boundaries are breached, the landmarks removed. Anything is possible if there is no God.

Our forefathers would be stunned to learn, for example, that the Constitution does not really mean what it says. The words they wrote were for another time. The document is "living and breathing" – which means that it is open to interpretation. Strict constructionists are ridiculed while politicians sneer at what they call "tyrannical consistency." It obstructs change and progress, they say. But if change is the rule, one wonders, who is to determine what version of change or progress is good?

When you strip the Constitution of its intent, its words, which its authors labored to write with precision and passion, you have discarded your heritage, replacing the Rule of Law with the whims of man. Now it's a jungle out there and each new day arrives with a fresh dose of scorn for our traditions and way of life. If the American people don't know—or care—about the Rule of Law, about the Constitution of the United States, then it's later than we think. As Bob Dylan would say, "The Titanic sails at dawn."

There was born a man in Prussia in 1818 whose life and influence would reshape the culture of nations and sound the death knell of freedom for millions. Few mourned the death of Karl Marx when he died in London, an atheist, penniless and stateless. Only eleven people attended his funeral. "His name and work will endure through the ages," eulogized his friend Friedrich Engels. The words seemed an unlikely boast, but he was right.

"Within a hundred years of his death half the world's population was ruled by governments that professed Marxism to be their guiding light," his biographer wrote. "His ideas transformed the studies of economics, history, geography, sociology and literature. Not since Jesus Christ has an obscure pauper inspired such global devotion.

Karl Marx is more popular today on most college campuses than Jesus. Writing in the *New York Review of Books*, on the attitudes and writings of America's elite scientists, Cambridge University Nobel laureate M. F. Peretz says, "Marxism may be discredited in Eastern Europe, but it still seems to flourish at Harvard."

Born to Jewish parents, both of whom converted to Christianity, Karl was baptized when he was six years old but would find little interest in the church. Headstrong and rebellious—and curious, he devoured Hegel, Voltaire, Proudhon, Immanuel Kant, Jean-Jacques Rousseau, Ludwig Feuerbach, and a long list of radicals. He and his wife Jenny had seven children, only three of whom survived to adulthood.

In Paris, he wrote for a radical German newspaper. When he expressed approval of the assassination attempt on Frederick William IV, King of Prussia, he was expelled. Next stop was Brussels, where he continued his studies and participated in a serious of rebellions and protests which led to his expulsion from Belgium. After brief stints in Cologne and a second time in Paris, Marx moved his family to London in 1849 where they would remain until his death in 1881.

His lifelong friend Friedrich Engels read the following statement at his funeral: "On the fourteenth of March at quarter to three in the afternoon, the greatest living thinker ceased to think. He had been alone for scarcely two minutes, and when we came back we found him in his armchair, peacefully gone to sleep—but forever."

His tombstone bears the carved message: WORKERS OF ALL LANDS UNITE and Engel's version of the 11th Thesis of Feuerbach:

> The philosophers have only interpreted the world
> in various ways—the point however is to change it.

Karl Marx spent his days and nights poring over the literature in the libraries and wrote some two dozen books, among them, *The Communist Manifesto* and *Das Capital*. He devoted his life to a systematic understanding of socio-economic change. The contradictions and inequities in capitalism necessitated its end, giving way to socialism. He had little love for the bourgeoisie (the class that, in contrast to the proletariat or wage-earning class, is primarily concerned with property values). They must be replaced by the proletariat (the class of workers, especially industrial wage earners, who do not possess capital or property and must sell their labor to survive).

Marx expressed this idea in the most famous sentence of Manifesto: "The workers have nothing to lose but their chains—they have a world to win." The idea was not to attain a new place in the old order of things, but to change the world itself. "It was about remaking the world. About going back to Eden and beginning again."

It's called socialism, class warfare. "From each according to his abilities, to each according to his needs." The government takes what you have earned, what you have acquired, what you own, and gives it to some else; they redistribute your wealth. It's not a return to Eden; in downhome vernacular, it's called stealing. It's a crime.

The philosophy, rooted in a lie, masquerading as caring and benign, has overturned the civil order of whole nations, plundered the wealth of millions, and turned cities and villages into cemeteries. It's a criminal enterprise that has failed wherever tried. "Every socialist state created by Marxists has been transformed into an economic sinkhole and a national prison," David Horowitz writes. "There are no exceptions." It has not led to utopia anywhere it has been tried but rather enslaved whole countries, reducing them to slave labor camps and police states. The Killing Fields of Cambodia are mute testimony to the horror that this "gospel" has wrought. Stalin's collectivization drive "to bring socialism to the countryside" was costly beyond imagination. As the Bolshevik leader Bukharin described it in his secret diary, the mass annihilation of completely defenseless men, women and children had transformed the comrades into "cogs in some terrible machine."

What is the reason for reviewing this historical nightmare? What does the retelling of the narrative have to do with the price of eggs at the market? The answer is clear: recounting the story underscores the importance of ideas. This radical politics has become "the intellectual currency of academic thought." It has tunneled its way into the universities. The universities are producing our politicians; and the politicians are writing the laws that affect and, some fear, threaten our future: "We won't have true justice until everything is equal in everybody's house," said a prominent spokesman of the Left.

Although it has been tried and found wanting, proponents of this pernicious system are now tenured professors in our universities, teaching this generation how to undermine the country that guarantees their freedom to express their hostility toward it.

The schoolmaster is Saul Alinsky, whose *Rules for Radicals* is no morality play. His influence in Washington today is disquieting. Alinsky is the godfather of a gaggle of politicians having learned well the art of doublespeak, prevarication, and expediency. Their modus operandi is not random; it is calculated, targeted and bereft of morality, and they make no bones about it.

Born to Russian-Jewish parents in Chicago in 1909, Alinsky was a Communist fellow traveler who spent his life on college campuses teaching young people how to organize the masses. In the first chapter's opening paragraph of *Rules,* Alinsky writes: "What follows is for those who want to change the world from what it is to what they believe it should be. *The Prince* was written by Machiavelli for the Haves on how to hold power. *Rules for Radials* is written for the Have-Nots on how to take it away."

Like Italy's Antonio Gramsci, Alinsky believed in working inside the system. He writes, "Any revolutionary change must be preceded by a passive, affirmative, non-challenging attitude toward change among the mass of our people. They must feel so frustrated, so defeated, so lost, so futureless in the prevailing system that they are willing to let go of the past and change the future."

He then codifies and writes a clear set of rules for community organizing, one of which is "You do what you can with what you have and clothe it with moral garments." Rule 12 is "pick the target, freeze it, personalize it, and polarize it."

Assessing the influence of Saul Alinsky, Jim Geraghty, a National Review Online contributor sums it up like this: "It's not about the policies or the politics, and it's certainly not about the principles. It's about power, and it has been for a long time."

Max Frankel thought he was onto something, a way to get around the hard choices, find new options. The executive editor of the New York Times from 1968 to 1994, Frankel declared in *Tikkun* magazine: "Ultimately, the solution to the Christian problem is simply to declare that God does not exist."

He continued, "I have grown certain that humanity invented God."

The only problem with that "solution" is that man is a creature. He was created. He is not autonomous, is not a self-contained unit of pride and excellence. Every breath he draws is borrowed. And being incorrigibly religious, he will have a god, if he has to make one. We're back to cracked cisterns again.

Wearied of the one true God, the Israelites made their own gods. The manufacture of gods became a virtual cottage industry.

> Therefore the king made two calves of gold, and said
> to the people, "It is too much for you to go up to Jeru-
> salem. This is your god, O Israel, which brought you
> up from the land of Egypt" (Exodus 32:4).

America, if you will not have the LORD God, then these are your gods—but a caveat: we tend to become like the gods we trust.

It will cost something to recapture the culture we once knew; to recover a sense of pride and dignity, the birthright of a free people; to restore God to His rightful place—Thou shalt have no other gods before Me—but it will cost much more if we do nothing.

The words of Ronald Reagan are as appropriate today as when first spoken:

> Freedom is never more than one generation away
> from extinction. We didn't pass it to our children
> in the bloodstream. It must be fought for, protected,
> and handed on for them to do the same, or one day
> we shall spend our sunset years telling our children
> and our children's children what it was like living in
> the United States when men were free.

6

The Sixties and Beyond

To understand the moral quagmire of the first years of the twenty-first century, we must revisit "the decade that changed America"—the 1960s.

"The stones we threw into the waters of our world in those days," Peter Collier has written, "caused ripples that continue to lap on our shores today—for better, and more often, for worse."

Syndicated columnist Cal Thomas agrees: "If you slept through the Sixties, you woke to a different America. It was the pivotal point of the recent past—an authentic decade of decision." Has any culture in history discarded its belief system as quickly as America did during that period? The rapidity with which we exchanged objective truth for a variety of subjective myths is both astonishing and frightening.

It might be worth noting at the outset of this chapter that the Sixties' radicals didn't go away; they took over. They donned three-piece suits and went to Washington. They became tenured professors in universities they once fire-bombed. They hijacked the once-proud profession of journalism and became firmly ensconced in the entertainment industry, using both as vehicles for their leftist and anti-American views. The social disintegration we are witnessing is the result. We are doing it to ourselves— and Toynbee reminds us that civilizations die by suicide not murder.

Shortly before his own death in 1861, Thomas Babbington Macaulay wrote a friend in America and said, "Your republic will be as fearfully plundered and laid to waste by the barbarians in the twentieth century as the Roman Empire in the fifth, with the difference that the Huns and Vandals who ravaged the Roman Empire came from without, and that your Huns and Vandals will have been engendered within your own institutions."

Something happened a generation ago that threw our world out of kilter and touched every facet of American life. The generation gap left families fractured and bewildered. Parents lost control of their children. Big government with bloated bureaucracies intruded on family life and private business. Courts struck down freedoms that had stood since brave men mutually pledged to each other their lives, their fortunes, and their sacred honor.

In 1787, 55 delegates gathered in Philadelphia to write a document that would define the future and secure the freedoms to our young republic. From thirteen colonies they came, possessed of a love of country, passionate patriotism, and a strong commitment to liberty. One hundred and 76 years later, another group met in another place to draft a document for a different purpose. Motivated by love for nothing but themselves, they were driven by hate—hate for the nation and contempt for its people. In his book, *Slouching Towards Gomorrah*, Robert J. Bork narrates this defining moment:

> The Sixties were born at a particular time and place: June, 1962, the AFL-CIO camp at Port Huron, Michigan. Though most Americans have never heard of the proceedings at Port Huron, they were crucial, for the authentic spirit of the Sixties' radicalism issued there. That spirit spread and evolved afterwards, but its later malignant stages, including violence, were implicit in its birth.

A small group of alienated, left-wing college students, calling themselves the SDS (Students for a Democratic Society), gathered together to change the world.

Their creed? "Four-square against anti-Communism, eight-square against American culture, twelve-square against sell-out unions, one-hundred-twenty square against an interpretation of the Cold War that saw it as a Soviet plot and identified American policy fondly."

"In short, they rejected America," Bork writes. "Worse, as their statement of principles made clear, they were also four-square against the nature of human beings and features of the world that are unchangeable." The Port Huron Statement drafted by Tom Hayden, was "a lengthy, stupifyingly dull manifesto with ignorance and arrogance proper to adolescents."

What was the SDS proposing? To use politics, "to bring their secular vision of the kingdom of God to fruition on earth, now." Bork explains: It is "an ideal that the most devout and active Christians have never remotely approximated for any community larger than a monastery, and probably not in any monastery." America was corrupt from top to bottom, and the Port Huron Statement sounded the alarm. It was a call to battle. These brave young soldiers would overturn the old order and trample on outmoded concepts like respect, reverence, order—even God. "It felt like the dawn of a new age," one of the SDS delegates said. "It was exalting. We thought we knew what had to be done and that we were going to do it."

The family was intact in 1960. There was little disagreement over its definition: husband and wife, with or without children. Today confusion reigns over the meaning of the "traditional" family. Radical feminist Betty Friedan claimed that families aren't dying or deteriorating, simply changing. She was quite explicit in her view that "we ought to get over our nostalgia for two-parent families headed by bread winner husbands , and deal with the reality of family in all its variety." Biological differences between men and women are relatively insignificant, external features. Everything is up for grabs; it's a new day. The family fared poorly in the Sixties and God didn't do so well either. The decade witnessed the most serious assault on religious freedom in our history. The Bible was thrown out of the schools, prayer became suspect in public places, and we witnessed the rise of militant secularism. When public officials in Washington, D.C. called for a day of prayer, an ACLU spokesman said, "It is always inappropriate for government officials to ask citizens to pray."

Before the 1960s, the idea that America was a Christian nation went virtually unchallenged. Before we knew what hit us, however, a blind rage against Christ and religion obscured the most salient facts of our tradition. One of the Chicago Seven, the militant atheist Abbie Hoffman, proclaimed. "God is dead, and we did it for the kids."

Herbert London, Professor of Humanities at New York University, was asked to serve as a TV commentator for a group of adolescents discussing teenage morality. "I pick and choose what I believe is right," said one of the participants. "My parents told me I am the best judge of what is moral." The teens could not agree that any behavior is wrong—except possibly murder, but not much else.

"Is it any wonder," London asks, "that we cannot deal with the moral chaos that surrounds us? The muscle of moral behavior has atrophied from disuse as many people—not only teenagers—pick and choose their preferred morality."

Patriotism has also taken a hit in the culture wars. I doubt that any classroom in America 50 years ago would have begun the day without the Pledge of Allegiance. Today the Supreme Court has designated the burning of the American flag a form of free speech. London expresses an appropriate concern when he writes:

> I yearn for a time when family values and personal responsibility didn't have to be defined; when barbarism was routinely shunned. Those days may not return, but we would be wise to retrace our steps asking what went wrong and how we can recapture the moral and civic virtues of a less tortured era.

Retracing our steps may not be pleasant. They will lead through the needle-strewn jungle of Haight-Ashbury where flower children turned on and tuned out; the muddy fields of Woodstock, where young people, mesmerized by raucous music, sought for love in all the wrong places; and the Ivy League campuses, where brave university presidents surrendered to student activists who demonstrated their passion for peace by occupying buildings, bringing firearms on campus, destroying manuscripts of books, assaulting and kidnapping officials, and resorting to murder when necessary.

Intoxicated by a sense of their own moral purity and superiority, they might well have remembered the words of Edmund Burke:

> Men are qualified for civil liberty in exact proportion to their disposition to put moral chains upon their own

appetites. Society cannot exist unless a controlling power upon will and appetite be placed somewhere, and the less of it there is within, the more there is without. It is ordained in the eternal constitution of things that men of intemperate minds cannot be free.

It is essential to understand that the rebellion leading to the chaos in the 1960s has changed its cloak but not its character. Its unrestrained impulse to evil, differing in style but not in substance, has ripped the fabric of our culture. The damage may be repaired, but only if the effort is immediate and sustained.

Alan Bloom put his finger on the problem when he wrote in *The Closing of the American Mind*, "There is one thing a professor can be absolutely certain of: almost every student entering the university believes, or says he believes, that truth is relative." When absolute truth disappears, a fissure appears in the foundation of the moral order. As the gaping hole grows larger and larger it eventually swallows up the pillars upon which a stable society rests. What, then, is left? Colleges and universities that devalue truth, and jettison anything that reminds the student of the day before yesterday; and a student body ignorant of the price their forefathers paid for the very lecture halls they occupy.

While doing research for this book, I attended a debate at the Yale Political Union. When one young debater made a disparaging reference to capitalism and the free enterprise system, the audience erupted in thunderous applause. I could not help but think how hypocritical since most of these law students were there because some "capitalistic entrepreneurs"—namely mom and dad—had worked eighteen hours a day for twenty years to pay their tuition.

The decapitation of truth continues when sensible curriculum is substituted for feel-good subjects that merely encourage students in their adolescent rebelling against authority. A case in point is Stanford's cowardly capitulation to a mindless minority who objected to a course on Western culture:

> The university had a very popular required course in Western culture. The idea was that students should have at least a nodding acquaintance with the minds and works that have shaped the West and that constitute our heritage. But radicals and minorities objected both because Western culture should not be celebrated, being racist, sexist, violent, imperialistic, and not at all like those wonderful Third World cultures, and because the authors that were assigned—Aristotle, Machiavellie, Rousseau, Locke, and Shakespeare—were all white males.

What happened? Stanford revised the course. The white male authors were replaced by women and writers "of color" who were bitterly hostile to Western civilization. Judge Bork calls this kind of capitulation "a quota system for the curriculum." Too many colleges and universities have become clinics where students are treated like animals in a research lab, objects for experimentation. And what do students receive in return for the thousands of dollars invested? Instead of instruction that will prepare them for a future career, they are too often exposed to courses in meaningless trivia that make a mockery of higher education. You can graduate from many of our leading institutions of learning having never taken a course in the history of Western civilization, American or English literature, mathematics, natural or physical science.

Themes that form the core ideology of multiculturalism—race, class, gender, and sexual orientation—are no longer scattered through the curriculum but are now a dominant part of it. The prevalence of such themes does not substantially differ from one school to another. Students are forced to face the regime of political correctness at nearly every institution of higher learning. And what are the consequences of such substandard educational requirements? According to a Rand Corporation study over one half of a national sample of college upper class students were unable to perform cognitive tasks at a high school level.

To entrust our young people to teachers and professors who have become "facilitators" and "change agents," who ridicule the Bible; caricature traditional religious beliefs and standards of decency and virtue; and despise the country that provides greater freedom and more opportunity than any people has ever known, is homicidal. More than 30 years ago Jewish scholar Will Herberg described modern man as resident of a "metaphysical wasteland." As Herberg went on to explain:

> We are surrounded on all sides by the wreckage of our great intellectual tradition. In this kind of spiritual chaos, neither freedom nor order is possible. Instead of freedom, we have the all-engulfing whirl of pleasure and power; instead of order, we have the jungle wilderness of normlessness and self-indulgence.

If you slept through the Sixties, "the decade that changed America," you woke to a vacuum in our social world, an emptiness. The first thing you noticed was that truth is dead. With preferences replacing laws, facts don't matter anymore. Once transcendent values are removed there are no moral standards. Absent a point of reference, truth becomes a floating target, and the result is heart-breaking. A young woman, a punk rocker lamented, "I belong to the Blank Generation. I have no beliefs. I belong to no community, or anything like that. I'm lost in this vast, vast world. I belong nowhere. I have absolutely no identity."

It's called betrayal, the betrayal of a generation. Like thrusting the eaglet out of the nest before teaching it to fly, we have left our children with no single, given belief they could put their fingers on. "Exploring the edges and precipices of modern freedom they have fallen into their share of abysses." The world is not a safe place for these children of broken homes, broken churches, broken governments; believing nothing is sacred and everything is profane, our kids are lost, just lost.

Carl Henry paints a grim picture:

> This generation is lost to the truth of God, to the truth of divine revelation, to the content of His will, to the power of redemption, to the authority of His His word; and for this loss it is paying dearly in a swift relapse to paganism. The savages are stirring again, you can hear them rumbling and rustling in the tempo of our times.

This slide toward relativism has now reached the dictionary. On November 16, 2016, "post-truth" was named word of the year by the Oxford Dictionaries. Every year the Oxford Dictionaries review candidates for word of the year and then debate the merits of one that captures the ethos, mood, or preoccupations of that particular year. So it's official, truth is dead. Facts are passe; we're moving on.

In his 2006 book, *The Audacity of Hope*, Barack Obama wrote:

> Implicit in the constitution's structure was a rejection of absolute truth, the infallibility of any idea, ideology, theology or ism, any tyrannical consistency that locks future generations in a single and unalterable course of action.

When absolute truth becomes tyrannical consistency we've entered the world of fantasy. Welcome to the twilight zone. With the loss of truth we don't know who we are. No memory, no future. If it's old, throw it away, take it to Goodwill. Theologian Thomas Oden explains, "We have blithely proceeded on the skewed assumption that new is good, newer is better, and newest is best." What is the result? "We adore today, worship tomorrow, disdain yesterday and loathe antiquity."

Novelist Milan Kundera once said that if you want to destroy a country, destroy its memory. With truth gone, history is suspect; the past must be expunged. Now you understand this penchant for hating anything that is "old hat," or "traditional," or that reminds us of the day before yesterday. If the flag offends, rip it down. If statue or monument damage fragile sensibilities, destroy them. Rename the old college, deface the 200-year-old monument. How we got here is no longer important; what is important is who we are—but we're not sure who we are. Shall we empty the cemeteries, exhume dead bodies and scrutinize their DNAs? Where does it stop? Certain traditional values: monogamous marriage, the nuclear family, the right to life, the good of prayer and church attendance. Are these bad things? Have we lost our way? What have we gained by throwing overboard the moral compass? Are the streets safer, homes happier, children more secure? Edmund Burke long ago warned: "The desecration of the past is the first step in the destruction of the present."

Memory is an integral part of human life and something precious is lost when tangible links to the past are discarded. In the words of Nietzsche: "Is there no up and down left, who gave us a sponge to wipe away the horizon, must lanterns be lit in the morning hours; what sacred games will we need to invent?" It's called lost.

George Orwell's *Nineteen Eighty-Four* is required reading—but only for the stout of heart. In Orwell's masterful critique of the political structures of our time, Winston Smith learns that the past gone, the Department of Records took care of that.

> So you realize that the past, starting from yesterday
> has been actually abolished? Every record has been

destroyed or falsified; every book has been rewritten, every picture has been repainted, every statue and street have been renamed, every date has been altered. History has stopped.

"The past is erased, the erasure forgotten; the lie became truth." History has stopped, truth is dead, and now you understand the rising young star who speaks of his obsession to fulfill "this sense of personal destiny." He says he is

> trying to make sense of the human condition and how to live in a modern, ever-changing world—with a sense of how one deals with existentialism, or the extraordinary lengths that people go to, to fill up the void, if they're cognizant or conscious of the grand and terrible hole that we have in our souls.

This terrible hole in the human heart is the true dilemma of our time—of all time. The flower children of the Sixties tried but failed to make sense of the human condition in their time, and we're not doing much better in the first years of the twenty-first century. With immutable truth dead and buried; and history, revised, rewritten, and finally expunged, we might do well to listen to the words of John Baillie: "In proportion as a society relaxes its hold upon the eternal, it insures the corruption of the temporal."

7

As the Church Goes

When first visiting New England many years ago, I was both fascinated and curious. The harbors, hills and rolling countryside with its quaint villages and bustling cities proved irresistible. Again and again I returned to the cradle of American liberty. Crisscrossing the New World of our ancestors I sought out the old churches, studied the landmarks, visited historic sights, drove the back roads and searched the libraries; all the while, questions haunting me: Whatever happened to the America our forefathers established. What went wrong? Where did we turn aside?

The great colleges and universities, established for the training of young ministers, are now bastions of theological liberalism and social activism. The birthplace of our civilization has become a virtual graveyard for many churches and institutions of learning. How and why did unbelief take root in such rich soil? When did we turn, and why?

I felt I was onto something when I stumbled upon a book written by Henry Steele Commager, *The American Mind*. Though written by no friend of the gospel, for whom "religion was clearly as irrational as modern art," it made a lot of sense. It couldn't have been clearer. Four things happened that changed the face of America, according to Commager, and the most amazing thing is that all four factors had to do with the church. As the church goes, so goes the nation—and the world. That principle has never changed, though we so quickly forget. The late Robert L. Bartley, then editor of the *Wall Street Journal*, wrote, "For a half-century now intellectual life and the courts have been profoundly hostile to religion in any public manifestation. This is a sorrow, for it represents the republic turning its back on its own heritage."

Santayana observed that, "We do not nowadays refute our predecessors, we pleasantly bid them good-bye." We simply forget. That's why it is important to note the four things Commager says altered the course of the nation's history.

The first one describes the church as materially powerful but spiritually ineffective: *while religion prospered theology went slowly bankrupt.* "Certainly by every test but that of influence the church had never been stronger than it was at the opening of the twentieth century," Commager observes, "and its strength increased steadily, but the church was something to be 'supported,' like some aged relative whose claim was vague but inescapable."

The church itself confessed to a steady secularization is the second thing Commager cites, then comments, "as the church invaded the social and economic fields, it retreated from the intellectual. Philosophy, which for over two centuries had been almost the exclusive property of the clergy, slipped quietly from their hands."

The third factor contributing to an altered national landscape had to do with the schools. *No longer did the Protestant churches control higher education.* "In 1840 the president of every important college in the country was a clergyman or trained to the church; a century later no clergyman adorned the presidential chair of any of the leading institutions of learning."

Finally, with the church weakened and theology bankrupt, *religion increasingly became a social function rather than a spiritual experience.* What does that mean? It means that each new generation must experience for itself the life-changing power of the gospel. Absent that experience and relationship it forfeits its moral function and assumes, instead, a secular one. As a nation, are we willing to pay the price for that forfeiture?

8

Lost in the Temple

A lmost everyone was a Christian at the opening of the twentieth century," Commager asserts. "It was fashionable to
attend church, to have your name on a membership roll somewhere. It was good for business and if you were a politician,
church membership would look good on the profile. Christianity was such a part of the culture that most people took their
religious affiliation for granted."

Churches became big business. Bishops were often chosen
for their leadership skills rather than their spiritual qualities.
Religion prospered, but theology sadly went slowly bankrupt.
Like the twelve-year-old boy from Nazareth lost in the temple;
somewhere in the journey, God got lost. The study of the Triune

God, an analysis of His character and attributes, became less important than the functions and activities of the church. The trappings of religion had overshadowed the larger issue of the worship of the one true God.

Cornelius Plantinga, former president Calvin Seminary, asks a probing question, "Have you noticed that a fair number of Christians are not particularly interested in God?" A fair number of Christians would be strangers to the heart-cry of the psalmist: "As the deer pants for the water brooks, so pants my soul for You, O God. My soul thirsts for God, for the living God" (Ps. 42:1, 1).

The Westminster Catechism was a staple in the intellectual and spiritual diet of the children for hundreds of years. Question: *What is the chief end of man?* Answer: *Man's chief end is to know God and fully to enjoy Him forever.*

Question: *What is God?* Answer: *God is a spirit, infinite, eternal,* unchangeable, *in His being, wisdom, power, holiness, justice, goodness and truth.*

In a humble carpenter shop in Nazareth two thousand years ago, Jesus learned what Jewish children had been taught for fifteen hundred years before: "Hear, O Israel: the LORD, our God, the LORD is one! You shall love the LORD your God with all your heart, with all your soul, and with all your strength" (Deut. 6:4, 5).

Theology is all about God and the failure or refusal to acknowledge and worship Him is the very definition of sin.

And even as they did not like to retain God in their knowledge, God gave them over to a debased mind to do those things which are not fitting; being filled with all unrighteousness, sexual immorality, wickedness, covetousness, maliciousness: full of envy, murder, strife, deceit, evil-mindedness; they are whisperers, backbiters, haters of God, violent, undeserving;

who knowing the righteous judgment of God, that those who practice such things are worthy of death, not only do the same but approve of those who practice them (Rom. 1:28-32).

No power on earth can stop a man from becoming reprobate if he rejects God. The mind that will not worship God becomes corrupted. It is impossible to understand our world as it is today without accepting the biblical diagnosis: "When they knew God they did not glorify Him as God . . ." Spiritual degeneration is the inevitable outcome. Sin leads to individual and collective ruin. Sin guarantees the breakdown of all human social systems; and there is only one solution for this breakdown: Worship. To know God, to fully enjoy Him, is our highest command and greatest pleasure.

To whom then will you liken God? To what likeness will you compare Him? "What comes into our minds when we think about God is the most important thing about us," said A. W. Tozer.

Theology is all about God. "In the beginning God created the heavens and the earth" (Gen. 1:1). Job: "O, that I knew where I might find Him" (Job 23:3). The psalmist: "O God, You are my God; early will I seek You; my soul thirsts for You; my flesh longs for You in a dry and thirsty land where there is no water" (Ps. 63:1). Moses: "LORD You have been our dwelling place in all generations. Before the mountains were brought forth, or ever You had formed the earth and the world, even from everlasting to everlasting, You are God" (Ps. 90:1).

Paul: "He is the image of the invisible God, the firstborn over all creation. For by Him all things were created that are in heaven and that are on earth, visible and invisible, whether thrones or dominions or principalities or powers. All things were created through Him and for Him. And He is before all things, and by Him all things consist" (Col. 1:15, 16). Peter: "Come to Him as to a living stone, rejected indeed by men, but chosen by God and precious" (1 Peter: 2:4).

John: "Then I turned to see the voice that spoke with me. And having turned I saw seven golden lampstands, and in the midst of the seven lampstands One like the Son of Man. . . . And when I saw Him, I fell as His feet as dead" (Rev. 1:12, 13, 17).

This is theology—the pursuit, the longing, the panting after God, as the deer pants for the water brooks. The 16th century Genevan Reformer, John Calvin, said, "Our hearts are idol factories and our words and actions are shaped by the pursuit of things our hearts crave." When we entertain other gods, or simply render the LORD God irrelevant, spiritual and moral insolvency ensues, individually and collectively. The business of religion may be noisy and exciting—or solemn and staid, but absent the living God, it is empty and vain, and its vanity is our shame.

Something happened to reality between the early 1800s and today. Liberal theologians, enamored with German "higher criticism," undermined the authenticity and authority of the Scriptures. Then along came Charles Darwin with his theory of evolution, which set the stage for the enemies of the gospel to seize control of public education and infiltrate the universities. The assault did not end until the pulpits of the land had been emasculated by clergymen who no longer believed what their congregations were paying them to preach.

We have noted before in these chapters that Darwinism changed the world; it tainted science, religion, psychology, philosophy, law; no discipline was left untouched. "The impact of Darwin on religion was shattering." Henry Commager comments. "Evolution banished the absolute, supplanted special design, challenged not only the Scriptural story of creation but creation itself, and revealed man not as the product of beneficent purpose but of the process of natural selection that, by denying the interposition of the Deity, confounded the concept of omnipotence."

The introduction of liberal theology is one of the sad chapters in our history; the wreckage is everywhere. Look at Union Theological Seminary. Charles A. Biggs took his doctorate at the University of Berlin under a professor of higher criticism that turned the New Yorker into a fiery apostle of German theology. His conversion to liberal theology was complete before returning to America. He caustically remarked that the Americans were far behind the times. He added that he now knew that his mission in life was to return to America and modernize theological studies in his own country. This he would attempt to do by disseminating German critical methods through our seminaries.

In his inaugural as head of the Department of Biblical Theology at Union Seminary on January 20, 1891, he said, "The Bible, as a book, is paper, print, and binding—nothing more. There is nothing divine in the text—in its letters, words, or clauses. He went on to say that "the Bible itself is the ghost of modern evangelicalism to frighten children."

His attack on the Scriptures was a turning point for a great seminary which went on to produce generations of gifted teachers and preachers who employed their gifts to cast aspersions on the Word of God.

The scar of theological liberalism is an earmark of the history of denominations in America today where it is fashionable to denigrate the Bible, having produced a generation almost contemptuous of anyone claiming to "know" anything. This flood of unbelief came "on a wave of irony and satire, exalting the trivial, ridiculing the noble and attacking anything which previous centuries had been taught to believe, revere, or love."

"Religion has lost all specificity and truth," said the atheist David Hume. "It is no more than a dim, meaningless and unwelcome shadow of the face of reason."

"We're storming the gates of heaven!" cried German socialist Karl Liebknecht at the end of WWI. "He need not have troubled," scholar and author Os Guinness said, "For most people, heaven had long since been evacuated and Man had come of age."

"Man makes himself," said Gordon Childe. "We see the future of man as one of his own making," said H. J. Muller. And Julian Huxley remarked, "Today, in twentieth-century man, the evolutionary process is at last becoming conscious of itself. Human knowledge, worked over by human imagination, is seen as the basis to human understanding and belief, and the ultimate guide to human progress."

It may not happen today or tomorrow, but at some point, with the loss of compass, the house of cards comes crashing down and you're buried in quicksand. There are no exceptions to that rule, though it may be disregarded in some quarters, ridiculed in others. The decline and fall of the great civilizations is profound confirmation of the reality that God will not be an addendum to man's story, for God is not mocked. Sin is transgression, striking out on your own; who needs God? And who is to define ultimate truth?

The dominoes start falling, and fall fast, when truth itself is compromised, given a different name, and assigned strange attributes. Which leads us to the ultimate issue in our search for the reasons for theology's demise. The first blow was struck when the Word of God was questioned. The first to go is the inerrancy of Scripture. "Forever, O Lord, Your word is settled in the heavens" (Ps. 119:89). "All flesh is grass and all its loveliness is like the flower of the field. The grass withers, because the breath of the LORD blows upon it. Surely the people are grass. The grass withers, the flower fades, but the Word of our God stands forever" (Isa. 40:6-8). "All Scripture is inspired of God and is profitable" (2 Tim. 3:16). "Knowing this first, that no prophecy of Scripture is of any private interpretation, for holy men of God spoke as they were moved by the Holy Spirit" (1 Peter 1:20, 21).

The first movement of Satan's interaction with mankind came with a sneer: "Yea, hath God said?" It was not a subtle, but blatant assault on God's Word, one that underlies all other slanders. Finessed as it passed through the seminaries, couched in technical terms as it filtered through the lecture halls, softened and sweetened as it mounted the pulpits, the stinging indictment persisted. The method of dispensing the lie may have been altered to suit the occasion, but the message was unchanged. Frontal attack or covert assault, the indictment was clear: God's Word is not to be trusted.

Dismissed as divisive and unnecessary by some, *The Battle for the Bible*, written by Harold Lindsell, hit the nail on the head. Lindsell was a Southern Baptist clergyman and former editor of *Christianity Today*. He served as vice president of Fuller Theological Seminary and was professor at Columbia Bible College. The theme of his book is biblical inerrancy, which he regards to be the most important theological topic of this age. "A great battle rages about it among people called evangelicals," he said.

He goes on to say that the he did not start the battle and wishes it were not essential to discuss it. "The only way to avoid it," Lindsell said, "would be to remain silent. And silence on this matter would be a grave sin." He chronicles the fall of religious denominations as well as colleges and seminaries, and notes with sadness how rejection of biblical inerrancy leads to denial of biblical truths that are inextricably connected with matters of faith and practice.

Lindsell cites Emory University as an example of an institution that betrayed its trust. Founded in 1836 as a Methodist school, it maintains its affiliation with the United Methodist Church, although it is unlikely John Wesley would feel at home there. Wesley wrote in his Journal, "Nay, if there be any mistakes in the Bible there may be as well a thousand. If there be one falsehood in that book it did not come from the God truth."

It was at Emory University that the atheist Thomas Altizer in 1975 announced the death of God. When officials were questioned about this, since the university was supposed to be Christian, the president defended Altizer. He taught that the "death of God is an historical event, that God has died in our cosmos, in our history, in our existence." He said he hoped the new Death-of-God School of theology would "give support to those who have chosen to live as Christian atheists."

Harold Lindsell points to a number of evangelical schools that at one time were on a platform, but are now on a slope, "and a slope soon becomes a slide, and it does not take long for people and institutions to hit the bottom." He appeals for an unswerving commitment to the trustworthiness of the holy Scriptures, and warns, "I am saying that whether it takes five or fifty years, any denomination or parachurch group that forsakes inerrancy will end up shipwrecked."

There is no alternative; if theology is bankrupt, religion may prosper, but the foreclosure of the church is just a matter of time.

9

Are We Yet Alive?

The genius of the church lies in its distinction—not isolation—from the world. Its effectiveness and power derive, in part, from its "other" worldliness; its strength has ever been its separateness; its attempt at syncretism, its downfall. The seeds of its own destruction were sown when it first sacrificed truth for unity. It went on life support when it sought to seduce the world only to be seduced by it.

Accompanied by tongues of fire and the sound of a rushing wind, the church burst onto the scene as Jesus had promised, "I will build My church and the gates of hell shall not prevail against it." The glory of this church has nothing to do with the world's applause. This world system will never embrace the church, understand its character, or approve its mission; and attempts by the church to curry the favor of the world by adjusting its position or watering down its message will simply incur further disdain for an institution unwilling to be true to itself.

Let us be clear: The coming of Christ into this world was more than a stop-gap measure or social justice enterprise. Jesus did not enter our world to apply band aids to its bleeding wounds but to shed His blood that He might permanently heal those wounds. And let it be noted in passing that the charge sometimes made that Christians are oblivious to the needs of their neighbors is a canard, as unfair as it is untrue. That the church does not care about the infirm or impoverished is groundless and does not accord with the facts.

Who over the centuries more than Christ and His church has striven in a thousand ways to improve the lives of people, building hospitals and orphanages and schools and soup kitchens? Nothing like that existed in the pagan world into which Jesus came. Every improvement of the lot of man on this earth has come directly or indirectly from the church. But that is not the principle reason Jesus came or why the church was born. He came to save sinners, and the mission of His church, while blessing everything in its path, is the gathering of the lost on its way into eternity.

Once that distinction is lost, that line breached, something happens to the essence of the church. Friedrich Schleiermacher sought to reach the "cultured despisers" in the nineteenth century, to engage them, to find some common ground. In principle, the effort should be praised. "A religion which totally abdicated the intellectual realm would soon lose almost all social influence and be confined to rather isolated pockets of uneducated people," James Hitchcock, author and scholar who taught at St. Louis University, writes in *What is Secular Humanism?* But Schleiermacher made two fatal flaws. The church "approached the skeptic, as it were, hat in hand, placing the church in a deferential and self-deprecating posture. It also took prevailing ideas in the secular intellectual world as normative, to which Christianity was expected to conform. The compromise was underway."

Hitchcock said, "In effect, Schleiermacher and his numerous religious descendants said, 'We will save as much of our faith as can be reconciled with secular thought. Having thus purified it, we hope that you secularists will agree to respect us.'" The folly—a folly with eternal consequences—of thinking the world will love us if we apologize for our faith or agree to water it down here or trim our sails there!

The word "liberal" found currency after the French Revolution, about the time Schleiermacher was writing, and it became common to speak of liberal Christianity. As Hitchcock notes, "Few words in the language are more slippery than 'liberal Christianity.' Once a good word, meaning to be generous; it came to mean an expansion of freedom, which in itself is not a bad thing. But as personal inquiry was exercised and encouraged, religious liberals frequently came to doubt, deny, or at least hold in suspension certain well established teaching of Christianity."

It is not hard to see how this drift once begun is difficult to control. Add to that the introduction of scientific findings in the nineteenth century, when debate raged over the age of the world, in the way in which it had been created, and other matters relevant to the physical sciences. Hitchcock argues that though some liberal professors were dismissed from seminary faculties, in the long run, in many denominations, they won the war.

One wall after another collapses when you start down that road. The first three chapters of Genesis are disputed, then other parts of the Bible are questioned, and once that thread is pulled the whole fabric unravels until finally you end up without firm conviction as to the nature of divine truth. Liberal theology empties the gospel of its power and you end up with bankrupt religion as theologian H. Richard Niebuhr describes it: "A God without wrath brought men without sin into a kingdom without judgment through the ministrations of a Christ without a cross."

James Hitchcock traces the progressions in liberal religious thinking, beginning with the earliest positions and moving to the present:

*While the Bible as a whole is inspired, certain passages not compatible with modern science, e.g., the creation accounts, are human inventions.

*While certain miracles central to the Christian faith, especially Christ's resurrection from the dead, must be believed, other miracle accounts in the Scripture are merely expressions of simple people.

*Christians must believe that Christ rose from the dead. However, they need not believe that the tomb was empty on Easter morning. The Resurrection can be understood as His continuing spiritual presence among his disciples.

*While Jesus was certainly the only begotten Son of God, secondary beliefs merely meant to reinforce that, e.g., His virgin birth, need not be believed.

*While God was certainly present in Jesus in a special way, it is not meaningful to speak of Him as the Son of God in the traditional sense.

*What is central to Christianity is the message of salvation brought by Christ and uniquely achieved through him. The circumstances of this redemption are subject to varying interpretations.

*To speak of man's being "saved" by Jesus presents problems since many people do not feel a need of being saved. Jesus is better seen as the greatest moral teacher in the history of the world and Christianity as the pinnacle of world religions.

*To regard Jesus as unique, and his teaching as superior to that of other religious leaders like the Buddha, is arrogant cultural chauvinism. God reveals himself in every culture in different ways.

*Whatever one may think about the various religions of the world, what is crucial is to believe in an all-powerful God who created the universe and sustains it in being.

*The word "God" is one which men have used through history to refer to some ultimate reality which is the deepest dimension of existence. Personalization of God and talk about His being creator and lord of the universe, are merely means men have used to make that awareness more vivid to themselves.

"In effect," Hitchcock argues, "the liberal strategy, far from enabling the core of Christian belief to stand out more brightly as accretions are stripped away, has made the whole of Christianity merely a series of accretions, fated to be given up one by one. Having abandoned any belief in ultimate religious authority in favor of a belief primarily in the efficacy of personal searching, liberals have no basis for remaining faithful to even the most fundamental Christian doctrines."

The original Methodist, John Wesley, once said, "I am not afraid that the people called Methodist should ever cease to exist either in Europe or America. But I am afraid lest they should exist only as a dead sect, having the form of religion without the power. And this undoubtedly will be the case unless they hold fast both the doctrine, spirit, and discipline with which they first went out."

We've come a long way from those days when Wesley exhorted his preachers: "You have nothing to do but to save souls. Therefore spend and be spent in this work." United Methodism has lost more than two million members in the past decades, the greatest loss in so short a period ever sustained by an American denomination. And they are not alone.

From New York to California the poison taints the bloodstream of the religious world. In Glide Memorial Church in San Francisco, where Gypsy Smith once called sinners to repentance, the Reverend Cecil Williams has garnered national headlines for its unorthodox blending of rock music, light shows, and its own version of "liberation theology." In 1967, Williams removed the cross from the church sanctuary saying "it was a symbol of death and that his congregation should instead celebrate life and living." He said, "We must all be the cross."

When questioned about moral issues, the pastor said, "I guess the important thing with me is that I don't become captive to the Scriptures. . . .I know somebody will say this is the inspired Word of God. But who has that kind of direct pipeline? Nobody." George Matheson had that kind of direct access and was happy to live under divine authority. In one of his hymns he has this line, "Make me a captive, Lord, and then I shall be free."

In *Paul's Attitude to Scripture*, E. Earle Ellis tells how an admirer once said to Adolf Schlatter, the renowned New Testament scholar, that he had always wanted to meet a theologian like him who stood upon the Word of God. Schlatter replied, "Thank you, but I don't stand on the Word of God; I stand under it."

Ellis comments, "He wasn't quibbling about prepositions. The distinction he made is a crucial one, and it goes to the heart of our discipleship as servants of the Word."

Overt apostasy is one thing; we have come to expect it, but we are troubled when methods, practices, doctrines (or lack of doctrinal specificity) alien to the heart of the gospel appear in evangelicalism. Distortions of the church's explicit message, diversions from its central purpose, distractions from its mission, if allowed to go unchecked, will rob the church of its edge, render it spiritually impotent, and leave it ultimately useless as an instrument of grace in the hand of the Lord.

Something tragic happens when religion becomes man-centered rather than God-centered. In juxtaposing the two, neither is God honored nor man elevated; man is debased and God is dishonored, and displeased. A great many unauthorized changes are threatening to weaken the church at a time when it ought to be speaking clearly, precisely and powerfully into the fog and blur of 21st century religion. The church has been assigned to go into all the world and preach the gospel to every creature. The nature of that gospel to be preached is explicitly spelled out in Scripture and is not open to debate.

"One thing is sure: if Bible-believing Christians neglect the primary purpose of Christ's entrance into history, there are no others who will take up the cause," Richard Halverson says. He appeals to the church to maintain its high calling while answering the critics who suggest the church should be in the business of social progress. Because evangelicals have been accused of neglecting social responsibility in their commitment to the gospel, "there is certainly no justification for neglecting the gospel in their zeal for social causes which have their ultimate resolution in the proper application of the gospel. The life and ministry of Jesus established the model."

Helmut Thielicke was one of the most effective preachers in Germany following the World War. He wrote a remarkable book about Charles Spurgeon, the prince of preachers who at the end of the nineteenth century—"when preaching had lost its popularity, when modernism, naturalism and humanism had reached the zenith of their influence, when theology had been downgraded to sub-zero, when nobody took sermons seriously—was preaching to 6,000 people every Sunday morning in London."

It was not the aim of this preacher to show people that their life would be easier if they accepted the gospel; that it would solve their problems; that civilization would perish without Christianity; that the state and society needed religion; that the Christian social ethic is absolutely indispensable; that the world order needs Christian foundations; that if our world is to endure there must be a renaissance of the Christian West. We stand in need of the simple way in which Spurgeon dares to say that what really ultimately counts is to save sinners. Indeed what really counts is that we get to heaven. Anything else is watered-down gospel, twaddle—including all the talk about the Christian West.

"The Bible was written in tears," A.W. Tozer noted, "and in tears it will yield its best treasures. God has nothing to say to the frivolous man." He cites Moses, "a trembling man," to whom God spoke on the mount, refers to Daniel's long season of prayer and fasting, and depicts John weeping because no one was found worthy to open the seven-sealed book. Tozer concludes, "Those Christian leaders who shook the world were one and all men of sorrows whose witness to mankind welled out of heavy hearts. There is no power in tears per se, but tears and power ever lie close together in the Church of the First-born."

Tears were a hallmark of the early church, and a seriousness, sometimes missing in our breezy convocations, characterized the men and women who through the centuries jeopardized their lives for the gospel. To reduce this holy business to fun and games is a snare. Entertainment was not a priority in the catacombs. To handle sacred things with careless hands is to risk the fate of Nadab and Abihu who offered strange fire to the Lord. To introduce cheap and tawdry performance in the house of prayer does not become sinners saved by grace.

Look at the record: "Therefore watch, and remember that for three years I did not cease to warn everyone night and day with tears" (Acts 20:31). "I tell the truth in Christ, I am not lying, my conscience also bearing me witness in the Holy Spirit, that I have great sorrow and continual grief in my heart. For I could wish that I myself were accursed from Christ for my brethren, my countrymen according to the flesh" (Rom. 9:1-3). "Who, in the days of His flesh, when He had offered up prayers and supplications, with vehement cries and tears to Him who was able to save Him from death . . ." (Heb. 5:7). Jeremiah wept for Josiah. Samuel wept all night for Saul. At the grave of Lazarus, as recorded in the shortest verse in the Bible, "Jesus wept" (John 11:35).

Witness the passion: "Now when they heard this, they were cut to the heart, and said to Peter and the rest of the apostles, 'Men and brethren, what shall we do?" (Acts 2:37). "Then Festus cried with a loud voice, 'Paul, you are beside yourself! Much learning is driving you mad!'" (Acts 26:24). "Agrippa said to Paul, 'You almost persuade me to become a Christian'" (Acts 26:28).

And the warnings: "I did not cease to warn everyone night and day with tears" (Acts 20:31). "I do not write these things to shame you, but as my beloved children warning you" (1 Cor. 4:14). "Christ in you, the hope of glory. Him we preach warning every man and teaching every man in all wisdom" (Col. 1:27, 28).

Those holy, radical followers of Jesus who turned the world upside down, lived their entire lives, faces set like a flint, pressing toward the goal for the prize of the upward call of God in Christ Jesus. There were no second thoughts about offending the world; the world had crucified the Savior. Their only concern was displeasing the Lord, standing one day at the bema judgment unprepared. The question we face today is are we yet alive or have we reduced the cross to yesterday's news; have we settled for performance rather than experience; or shall we insist on the invasion of our lives by a new quality of life altogether described as Christ "living in" us?

"We have to recover our prophetic stance," insists Car. F. H. Henry. "We have to refuse to succumb to the lure of being included with all the other important people. Prophets do not get invited to prayer breakfasts. There is a time and place where we refuse to sell ourselves for seats at the supposed positions of power in order to affirm our distinctives. We need to keep in mind that there is no guarantee of fame or success in our faithful proclamation. We so often measure faithfulness by fame, but in biblical faith the call to integrity comes without a supporting cast of wealth or public recognition."

The secularization of the church at the beginning of the nineteenth century was a turning point. Tongues of fire, the sound of a rushing wind, bold proclamation—this belonged to another time, to another day; abandoning their original passion and purpose, the people of God instead preached relative and secondary values. A secularized church in Germany in the 1930s and '40s, which became a silent church, contributed to the horror of the Second World War and provides a lesson for American Christians today. Are we yet alive, or have we reduced the story of the cross to yesterday's news, settled for performance rather than experience, or shall we insist on the invasion of our lives by a new quality of life all together described as Christ *living in* us?

10

When the Church Was Silent

Many Germans were anxious to walk away from the years of terror and brutality that had turned their nation into one giant death camp. Two short decades after the collapse of the Third Reich, statesman Willy Brandt—himself a "good" German and never a Nazi—told a cheering crowd of 400,000 Berliners that "twenty years is enough. We shall not be ashamed for these years."

"We do not believe in collective guilt," Elie Wiesel said, "but we are responsible for the way we remember the past." Every faithful Jew knows the ring of that word: remember. Remember that you were slaves in the land of Egypt. Remember the day in which you came out of Egypt. Remember what Amalek did to you. Remember the days of old, consider the years of many generations.

Survivors of the ghettos and the camps are growing older, their numbers diminishing, and there are none to come after them. They meet at funerals now, but they are determined to remember. They are witnesses and they will not be silent. To suggest otherwise is to insult those who perished under the whip, in burning pits, on the gallows and in the ovens. The passage of six decades has not eased the pain or erased the memories. "To forget would mean to kill the victims a second time," Wiesel argues. "We could not prevent their first death; we must not allow them to be killed again."

General Dwight Eisenhower was furious at what he saw upon liberating Dachau. The Supreme Commander of the Allied Forces ordered that photographs be taken and that people from surrounding villages be ushered through the camp, because "somewhere down the track of history, someone will get up and say this never happened."

Could the Holocaust happen again? That question can best be answered by posing another: Could the Holocaust have been prevented? "Quite possibly," Juda Pilch answers, "but no one really tried."

In *The World Was Silent*, Pilch raises some troubling questions: "Why was the civilized world silent and why did the churches not raise their voices on behalf of the Jews?"

He cites the inaction of governments. "These are the facts," he writes. "More than two million Germans were directly connected with the Nazi machinery of destruction, and many more millions profited from the pillage and loot. The masses of the German and Austrian populations knew of the ant-Jewish measures . . . yet the vast majority of Germans were silent."

Their silence was deafening when they heard brownshirted fellow Germans singing: *Wenn das Judenblut vom Messer spritzt, dann geht's noch mal so gut* (When Jewish blood drips from the knife, then things are twice as good).

Dr. Karl Jaspers, the German philosopher, spared no words when he addressed the World Jewish Congress held in Brussels in August 1966: "When our Jewish friends were taken away, we did not go down into the street, we did not cry out until we, too, were exterminated. We preferred to remain alive, alleging—truthfully but weakly—that our death would not have made any difference."

The indifference of the Poles to the persecution of their three and a half million Jews was heartbreaking, but not surprising. In their hatred of their Jewish neighbors they said, "Let the Germans do this dirty job for us." Driven by the centuries-old climate of anti-Semitism, they were only too ready to acquiesce to the terror and tyranny that allowed Poland to become the slaughterhouse of the Jews of Europe.

It cannot be denied that the silence of the world contributed to the events leading up to World War II. Nor can anyone plead ignorance with regard to Hitler's intentions. He made no bones about what he planned to do. "For whatever other accusations can be made against Adolf Hitler," William L. Shirer, author of *The Rise and Fall of the Third Reich*, asserts, "no one can accuse him of not putting down in writing exactly the kind of Germany he intended to make if he ever came to power and the kind of world he meant to create by armed German conquest."

The aspiring Nazi leader spelled it out in *Mein Kamph*, the book of some 400 pages written while incarcerated in 1924 following the failed beer hall putsch, the ill-fated attempt to overthrow the government. Placed under arrest and confined in the old fortress at Landsberg, he bided his time, dictating in chapter after chapter a blueprint of the Third Reich, and of the barbaric New Order he would impose on conquered Europe.

Three editors were required to wade through the heavy,

turgid prose of the first volume, and the second, completed in 1926, bringing the total pages to 782, correcting bad grammar and making sense out of the author's random thoughts on almost every conceivable subject. The book outsold everything but the Bible during the Nazi regime, was an appropriate gift for any occasion, and was presented to school children upon graduation. The politically correct thing to do was own a copy and display it in office or home, although it is not certain how many Germans made it through to the last page, it being a rather cumbersome reading assignment. What is clear is that Hitler made no attempt to conceal his fierce nationalism, his hatred of democracy and Marxism, and especially the Jews.

"I do not look upon Jews to be animals," he wrote. "They are further removed from the animals than we are, therefore it is not a crime to exterminate them since they do not belong to humanity at all."

It strains credulity to believe that anyone having read *Mein Kamph* should have been surprised when storm troopers began roaming the streets, rounding up victims; onerous laws restricting civil liberties were enacted; borders were crossed and bombs dropped; Jewish shops were vandalized, their owners and patrons beaten; and when shooting and clubbing them to death grew monotonous, gas chambers and crematoria were invented to speed up the solution to the vexing "Jewish problem."

The extent and virulence of the brutality unleased during the reign of the Nazi regime may have shocked some gentle folk, but they should not have been surprised. The cost of the failure to read the writings of this madman and grasp the implications they conveyed was simply catastrophic; destruction of economies, of businesses, home and infrastructure; widespread use (and abuse) of slave labor and creation of extermination camps; bombing and burning of the great cities of Europe; new kinds of terror and torture; mass murder on a scale unprecedented; in short, a cataclysmic rupture of human life from the Atlantic to the Urals.

In "the blueprint of what the Almighty had called upon him to do," Hitler telegraphed his intentions to the world. He outlined his vision of the future of Germany and what was required to make it a reality. Hitler had a couple of favorite words. One was *Weltanschauung* (and the other was *Lebensraum*), a view of life; a point of view, the window by which one views the world. Authoritarianism would define the German Reich:

"There must be no majority decisions, but only responsible persons. . . . Surely every man will have advisers by his side, but the decision will be made by one man . . . only he alone may possess the authority and the right to command. . . . It will not be possible to dispense with Parliament. But their councilors will then actually give counsel. . . .In no chamber does a vote ever take place. They are working institutions and not voting machines. This principle—absolute responsibility unconditionally combined with absolute authority—will gradually breed an elite of leaders such as today, in the era of irresponsible parliamentarianism is utterly inconceivable."

There must be no question as to the character of the new German government, Hitler wrote, if it was to erase the shame of defeat in the Great War and recover its position as a world power. "The great questions of the day," Bismarck declared in becoming prime minister of Prussia in 1862, "will not be settled by resolution and majority votes—that was the mistake of the men of 1948 and 1849—but by blood and iron." Blood and iron, a willingness to trample on one's closest friends; a willingness to "crush people with the boots of a grenadier."

Hitler would be that man. "When brutality was called for, he could act with force and decisiveness," the French would later learn. There was little love lost between France and Germany. Legend has it that George Clemenceau, prime minister of France during the Paris Peace Conference, asked to be buried upright, facing Germany, mute testimony to his mistrust of the neighbor to the east. Clemenceau was a young man when the French armies were defeated in the Franco-Prussian War and he never forgot, his country decimated, people starving in the streets. Shortly before his death, he told an American journalist that his life hatred had been for Germany because of what it had done to France.

Hitler returned the favor, reciprocated that hatred, referring to France as "the inexorable mortal enemy of the German people." The French aim, he said, would always be to achieve a "dismembered and shattered Germany. . .a hodgepodge of little states. Therefore, there must be a final reckoning with France. . . a last decisive struggle. . . only then will we be able to end the eternal and essentially fruitless struggle between ourselves and France; presupposing, of course that Germany actually regards the destruction of France as only a means which will afterward enable her finally to give our people the expansion made possible elsewhere."

Expansion. *Lebensraum*—living space. A map of Europe finds Germany cramped and crowded, nearly landlocked with insufficient room for its 75 million people. France has 40 million occupying the same amount of land, if not slightly more. Look at the vast stretches of land to the eat. Hitler coveted the soil occupied by the Poles, the Slavs and the Russians. In the first place, he despised the Poles: "The men capable of leadership in Poland must be liquidated. Those following them must be eliminated in their turn. There is no need to burden the Reich with this."

The Slavs were little better. As for the Russians, they didn't need that much space. Hitler believed that "the soil exists for the people which possesses the force to take it." If the present possessors object? "Then the law of self preservation goes into effect; and what is refused to amicable methods, it is up to the fists to take." The push must be resumed for a new and expanded Reich. "We must hold unflinchingly to our aim . . .to secure for the German people the land and soil to which they are entitled." Hitler lays it all out in *Mein Kamph*. There are no secrets here. This is what the future holds, if anyone cares to listen; and the man dictating these chapters will make it happen.

Time after time he would defy the world, dare anyone get in his way. He despised the old men of the Weimar government in Berlin, whom he would replace, and was contemptuous of the little men who had gone to Paris in 1919, "to do nothing less than fix the world."

David Lloyd George, Woodrow Wilson, the Italian Prime Minister Vittorio Orland, Lawrence of Arabia, "wrapped in mystery and Arab robes," together with other world leaders, had descended on the French capital and for six months had labored to repair the old continent that had been torn to pieces in the First World War. The Treaty of Versailles would create a world "safe for democracy," and the starting point would be the imposition of some harsh reality on Germany, a major culprit in the war. For starters, reparations were demands. In a further insult, Germany's military capability was to be severely restricted, reducing the army to something like a police force with "no air force, tanks, armored cars, heavy guns, dirigibles and submarines." Weaponry along the disputed Rhine was to be deeply cut or destroyed.

The peace conference ended. Presidents and prime ministers who had made long speeches, argued, debated, quarreled and made up again, returned home. New nations had emerged and great empires had died. Now it was over, the grand scheme to form a League of Nations set on a course away from war toward peace and brotherhood. Woodrow Wilson went home to face a hostile Senate which had determined to torpedo the whole thing, and failing to gather the support of the American people suffered a stroke and died. Lloyd George lasted two more years in office, and Clemenceau was soon gone. Meanwhile, "the little corporal" from Austria was on his way toward becoming master of Europe.

Embarrassed by defeat in the war and humiliated by the injustice (in their view) of sanctions imposed by the victors, it was time for Germany to settle some scores. The first order of business: rebuilding the decimated military capability. On October 1, 1934, Hitler ordered troop levels increased from 100,000 to 200,000. In March the following year, the chancellor established military service and a peacetime army of half a million men. Two battle cruisers of 26,000 tons (16,000 tons above Versailles limits) were ordered. And what are these dashing sky-blue uniforms? They are the uniforms of the German Air Force. But there was to be no Luftwaffe. A few protested, but did not act. So much for the military restrictions of Versailles.

One of the most contentious issues arising during the Paris Peace Conference was the question of the Rhineland, that narrow strip of land along the river "which had always been a barrier between Western civilization and something darker, more primitive." It was decided after long and bitter debate, that the Rhineland was to be demilitarized, with Britain and the United States occupying it for fifteen years, and Germany prohibited from ever going there again.

That was then. Against the better judgment of his generals, on March 7, 1934, a small contingent of German troops crossed the Rhine bridges and entered the demilitarized zone. "The German Minister of Defense had given orders for his troops to withdraw across the Rhine, should the French move to oppose them," Shirer notes, "but the French never made the slightest move. Had France protested, as they were capable of doing, that almost certainly would have been the end of Hitler, after which history might have taken quite a different and brighter turn than it did, for the dictator could never have survived such a fiasco. Hitler himself admitted to as much: 'A retreat on our part,' he conceded later, 'would have spelled collapse.'" Colonel Alfred Jodl testified at Nuremberg, "Considering the situation we were in, the French covering army could have blown us to pieces."

For France, it was the beginning of the end. The rape of

Austria was followed by the seizure of Czechoslovakia, and, then, Poland. "At daybreak on September 1, 1939, the German armies poured across the Polish frontier and converged on Warsaw from the north, south and west."

Even at this dark turn, the world standing on the threshold of its bloodiest war, neither London or Paris issued a word of protest, or lifted a finger to honor their commitment to Poland. And at what cost? How many times must it be said, and in how many ways, that there is one thing worse than a cultured people committing genocide, and that is a cultured world remaining silent in the face of genocide?

Even the churches were silent. "An even more painful question," Judah Pilch writes, "is the silence of organized religion. No official representations were ever made by the heads of the Christian churches which could have expressed in the strongest possible terms the protest of all true believers. While the death factories operated at full blast, the papacy itself was silent. No attempt was made to mobilize the resources of the world's religious institutions for the defense of Nazi victims."

The failure of the German churches to resist, to cry out, to open their homes, to shield Jews from the terror of *Kristallnacht*, for example, is a stain that will not go away.

This *is* Germany, after all. The great Reformation sprang from this soil. It was here Martin Luther nailed his 95 theses to the Wittenberg Door. It was here he struck a blow for the freedom of the gospel, defying popes and priests and heralding a new day for *Sola Scriptura* (The Scripture Alone) and *Sola Fide* (Justification by Faith Alone).

How could the church have failed here, where the Gutenberg Press had printed a Bible for the masses; where the Book of Romans, unshackled from theory and tradition, and liberated from the musty shelves of monasteries, had broken the chains of a continent, then the world? How could descendants of Martin Luther, who once sang "A Mighty Fortress is Our God," have succumbed to the siren song of a harsh and demanding dictator who had no music in his soul?

The world is still trying to unravel the mystery surrounding the career of that unprecedented evil called Adolf Hitler, attempting to ascertain the reason for the world's acquiescence to his demands. We have already noted the repeated failure of European nations to rebuke Hitler's brazen trashing of the clear norms of international law. But where was the intellectual community? Why was academia silent? Where the professors, the pundits?

Where was the business community? Why were they so willing to turn a blind eye to Hitler's excesses? What deafened them to the cries of injustice and oppression? Is there no limit to the price conscience will pay for profit, or had they ever pondered the question: "Is life so dear, or peace so sweet, as to be purchased at the price of chains and slavery?"

But the church—heralder of good news, friend of sinners, supporter of the weak, the visible body of Christ—did not matter; there was no authoritative voice, the pulpits were silent. The cross of Christ had been exchanged for a broken cross. Sinai's thunder had fallen silent, reduced to a whisper, and the rushing mighty wind of Pentecost was but a memory. People still gathered in churches, sermons were preached, classes held, conferences organized; the busywork of religion must not be impeded by the broken windows of Jewish shops or the jailing of "undesirables."

The First World War had left the country broke. The Kaiser had sued for peace and fled to Holland, leaving his defeated countrymen to foot the bill. Economic loss, staggering unemployment, a broken armed forces, wounded national pride, rendered the country ripe for a leader—a strong leader, one who would make Germany great again. Out of the crucible of wild flights of fantasy, daydreams of greatness, boiling anger and resentment, street fights and imprisonment, such a leader emerged. He revived the economy, reduced inflation, stabilized the currency, created jobs, rebuilt the military, and restored a sense of pride and confidence in the people; Adolf Hitler made them proud to be Germans again. In 1937, Winston Churchill said that these achievements were "among the most remarkable in the whole history of the world."

But that was 1937. In an important book, *Hitler's Cross*, Erwin Lutzer, author and theologian, quotes one historian who suggested that if Hitler had died before World War II he would have gone down in history as Adolf the Great, one of the outstanding figures in German history.

"But Hitler didn't die before World War II," Lutzer reminds us, "he didn't die until the German people had surrendered their personal rights, until laws were enacted that led to the extermination of more than eight million people, and until Germany and several other countries were destroyed in a war that killed 50 million people in the greatest bloodshed in history. He didn't die until thousands of pastors joined the SS troops in swearing personal allegiance to him."

Hitler had made clear that one man would do what parliaments could not. Getting the trains running again, restoring economic viability, restarting the engine of national pride; that was a one-man job—and he was the man.

Hitler could not have achieved what he did without neutralizing the church. Dictators rule by fiat, brook no opposition; disloyalty only exists as long as it takes to load the gun. Other voices cannot be tolerated, especially when that voice says, "I am the LORD Thy God."

"Adolf Hitler knew that in order for his program to succeed," Richard Terrell writes in a serious book every Christian ought to read, *Resurrecting the Third Reich*, "he would have to 'deal' with the churches, either by unifying them with the Nazi ideology or disarming their power." This would require some patience. You don't summarily liquidate an institution like the church with roots burrowed deep in the soul of its nation psyche. Deception, seduction must be employed; confidence in the Word of God eroded.

Fortunately for the leader of the new Germany, the foundations for the distortion of the gospel had already been laid in the seminaries where the faith had been redefined. "By the time Hitler came to power," Terrell writes, "all the precedents had been set and all the philosophical principles had been established whereby a nationalistic idolatry could be substituted for the gospel of Jesus Christ."

William Horndern has noted "that for a century theologians had tried to modernize the faith by accommodating it to the modern age. Now, in Germany, Hitler was the modern age and thus it seemed logical to accommodate Christianity to this latest form of modernity." Nazism had become a parody of Christianity "with racialism substituted for God, and German 'blood' for Christ."

"Wolves had entered the German flocks," Lutzer says. "The church stood poised between two crosses, wanting to be loyal to both but learning that neither cross could tolerate the other. The church made peace with an enemy with which it should have been at war. Called to warn and protect, it tolerated, then saluted, then submitted."

Nina Altmon Katz, born in Sosnowiec, Poland, on May 24, 1929, whose story is recounted in the next chapter, is a witness to what happens when prophets and priests fail to warn and protect; when "good" people, confronted by a monstrous evil, tolerate, salute, and then submit.

11

Out of the Night

"The Germans are coming! The Germans are coming!" Cries of alarm spread from house to house in the Jewish community: "The Germans are here!" There had been rumblings and rumors for weeks but now a million and a half German soldiers had poured across the Polish border bringing with them a fierce wrath to be inflicted first upon the Jews.

The authorities would be of little help. Jews were hated in Poland almost as much as they were in Germany. The Polish people were something less than hospitable toward the Jews whom they called nasty names and taunted as "Christ killers." They were frequently victims of cruel discrimination in the markets and schools and on the street. Beatings were not uncommon. Wearing handsome velvet caps, college students threw rocks and broke windows of Jewish homes and waved banners, warning, "Prech Z Zydami!" (Away with the Jews). Even the Catholic Church got in the act; it made no effort to conceal its anti-Semitism. The faithful were taught how to properly treat these undesirables. The priests did their job well and the hatred they preached simmered throughout the country.

"Why do they hate us?" twelve-year-old Nina Altmon often asked her grandfather, a respected rabbi. "They are jealous, my child," he would say. "We are the chosen people. What do they know? You are special. God will take care of us." But where was God now with Nazis banging on the door, Polish citizens having pointed out Jewish homes? "Let them do the dirty work for us."

"Raus! Raus! Juden, out!" German soldiers shouted, their commands sprinkled with curses and threats. "Out, quickly, Jews, out!" Nina had the presence of mind and just enough time to rush to a drawer and snatch a handful of family pictures, hiding them in her skirt. Tucked away in the hem of her prison uniform, a black-and-white picture of her mother and father would sustain her through six years in two Czechoslovakian labor camps.

"We walked like robots," Nina said. "Simply terrified, we had no way of knowing what was happening to us." As they marched, others joined until the great company converged at the sports stadium near the railroad tracks.

"We waited here two days and two nights without food, water or toilet facilities." Nina painted a picture of abject horror: "I saw men hanging from trees. I saw a soldier seize a baby nursing at its mother's breasts, swing it around and dash its head against a wall. When the screaming mother, hysterical, protested, she was shot. They used the baby as a human football," Nina said, then in a half whisper, "I dream about that."

The family was separated, father, grandfather and little sister to the left; Nina and others to the right. She could not have known at the time that she was spared because she was a tall girl, of sturdy build. She could work. Older people and little children were sent immediately to extermination centers. They were of no use.

To the right and to the left, families were separated. Down the center corridor roamed brawling, drunken German soldiers with steel helmets and rifles cocked, shouting and cursing and shooting at will. What happened that day in Sosnowiec, Poland, seemed like a dress rehearsal for hell.

When the trains pulled up, Nina remembers running to a nearby school. "It had French windows, the kind that swing outward. I crawled up on the sill and searched for my family." There! There! When she spotted them, Nina yelled, waving and crying. "But they didn't see me; I would never see them again."

Childhood ended that day for the little Jewish girl and for thousands of others. Nina would become a teenager in a work camp, but there would be no celebration, no hugs from a little sister, no reassuring words from her grandfather; her teen years remembered for the sight of bodies of prisoners who had died in the night, the sensation of a living death by starvation, the gratuitous brutality and utter lack of the slightest hint of human kindness.

There's something about trains, a certain romance—the platform crowded with people awaiting the arrival of family or friends, others off on a business trip, or some adventure. There's a fascination about it: the sights and sounds, sweeping white light as the train approaches, the screeches and whistles. And always the movement. The earth trembles when the train arrives and you are momentarily deafened until it screeches to a halt, narrow plumes of smoke coming from somewhere. Passengers descend as others line up to take their places. There is wild commotion near the baggage cars as wagons move to exchange cargo—milk cans, mail bags, cardboard containers and wooden crates, and sometimes a coffin.

But there was no joyful anticipation in Sosnowiec that day in 1939, no greetings or smiles. There was no romance here as this train approaches, its deadly assignment about to begin. For there are no passenger coaches with soft seats. These are cattle cars with the smell of death upon them. Cattle cars, driven by hate, without sanitation or ventilation, without food or water, and not a modicum of concern for the welfare of its freight of brutalized, terrorized Jews whipped onto the cars with angry curses and violent threats.

Nina Altmon did not know that her family had gone to Auschwitz, nor did she know where she was going, or the extent to which her world had changed forever. "We were crammed into the compartments." Nina said, "There were some places where you could sort of peep out, but you couldn't see much. We didn't know where we were going. There were no toilet facilities, no food or water. We were all pushed in, children kept to the front, the adults pushed back against the wall. Wherever they stopped, they loaded on more people. It was one of those journeys I wish I could forget."

"The engine's whistle had an uncanny sound, like a cry for help sent out in commiseration for the unhappy load which it was destined to lead into perdition." Dr. Victor Frankl, internationally renowned psychiatrist, who lost his entire family in the camps, remembered the journey to Auschwitz.

Packed in a smelly cattle car, traveling through the Polish countryside at night, Nina had nothing now but the handful of pictures she clutched tightly—and the memories. Good food cooking on the potbelly stove, books, music, Grandfather's encouragement and careful instruction—and her sister Helen. Seven-year-old Helen, with that little girl smile. "She would wait for me at the gate when I came home from school. She was small and I was tall so she would hang onto me all the way to the house," Nina remarked wistfully.

"There were no clocks," Nina responds, when asked about the trip. "The doors were never opened except when we stopped to pick up more people. We must have traveled for two or three days; nobody came to inform us.

Nine remembers how difficult this trial was for older people. "I remember this man who couldn't breathe. 'Move aside,' everyone shouted, 'move aside, he needs air.' But there was no air.

"We hardly knew what to expect when we arrived at Hannsdorf labor camp where we would spend the next three years," Nina said. "Upon arrival, we were told to undress and put on prison garb with the star of David on front and back. Then the shrill and ugly threats began. We were told that when the whistle blew we would march to and from work. Roll call before dawn, a crust of bread, and the prisoners were off to the factory, marching in step, with a smack from a rifle if out of line. If we survived the day," Nina remembered, "we could look forward to another roll call at night and a cup of watery soup before climbing up to our beds, which consisted of boards covered with straw."

So what was a day like at Hannsdorf, the labor camp across the Czech border? "We worked in a spin factory where they made big spools of yarn. These spools were sent to another factory where they were made into a fabric, which went to the shops to make uniforms. It started out in the factory where I worked."

Nina described the procedure which required great care. "You had to have the eye of an eagle to see the thread . . . the minute a thread broke, they would yell 'sabotage' and somebody would be shot. We watched each other's back. People were shot right in front of us if a thread broke. I narrowly escaped being shot. Then it went through water and through the combs and eventually it started twisting. Before you knew it, it ran on another type of machine and made the yarn. That's what we did. It was dark when we left our bunks and it was dark when we returned. There were no clocks. Nobody told us anything."

When asked if she ever despaired of life, Nina recalled one

bitter winter. "We were wearing wooden clogs and a cotton prison uniform and a scarf on our heads and we were working in the snow. The bottom of my uniform was wet and we were hungry. We were cold. We kept asking each other why, what crimes have we done? So for us, the only solution was to die in our sleep. You couldn't commit suicide if you wanted to. Some died of malnutrition. Some winters the barracks were covered with ice and snow. The air was so cold and sharp. I have been to hell and back, and everyone else who survived will tell you the same thing."

Death was a constant in the camps. Nina recalls waking up one morning and shaking her partner, "time to wake up," then feeling her and discovering that she was frozen. When people died, they were buried in unmarked graves. "The graves are everywhere. Why some of us survived," Nina still wonders, "is beyond me. I don't know, but I felt I had a mission in life. I never gave up. As much as it hurt to see what was going on, we were determined that Hitler would not win."

Nina would spend the next three years in a concentration camp. "One morning, without warning, they said, 'Take your prison uniform and your apron and you will start marching.' How long we marched I do not know. We finally came to a railroad station where they pushed us into freight trains which took us to Oberalstadt, a concentration camp in Czechoslovakia. Security was extremely tight here with barbed wire everywhere."

The rations and endless hours of work remained the same. The beatings stopped at Oberalstadt, but the cruelty never ended. "I remember many times the SS would get us up in winter when the snow was up to our waist and say, 'Go out and get a bucket and drain the river.' They invented such beastly rituals. Civilized human beings could never think of such things."

Nearby was a camp of British prisoners of war. The Brits would come out in the middle of the night, wrap a note around a stone and throw it over the fence. The message was always the same: "Don't give up hope, freedom is near."

But hope seemed illusive, freedom far away. "How many times I prayed during those years, 'take my soul and let my sufferings be over.' I often despaired, thinking I couldn't endure another day."

It is not pleasant for the chronicler, whose assignment it is to record these events. For the survivors, it is not simply unpleasant. To be reminded of this period in their lives is to relive the nightmare. More sleepless nights, more anguish, and the incessant demand for answers. Why, then, inflict such pain on writer and reader? The answer is clear: "Six million were wiped off the face of the earth," writes the esteemed interpreter of the prophets, Abraham Joshua Heschel, "and there is danger that they will be annihilated from our memories. Are they doomed to a twofold annihilation?

Much of the material in this chapter is shocking and ugly. No effort has been made to whitewash the narrative, to gloss over the reality. Holocaust deniers and the passage of time tend to blur the picture, to obscure the obscenities, to make them go away. But they won't go away. The great Jewish historian Shimon Dubov said over and over to his community in the Riga ghetto, "Jews, write it all down."

"Even if you survive, even if you tell, no one will believe you," an SS told a young Jew somewhere in Galicia. He was wrong. Nina Altmon and her fellow survivors are witnesses. They will not go away, and they will be heard; in poems, in lectures, in memoirs and documents of all kinds. Their major preoccupation is memory. They are witnesses and they will not be silent.

Nina shares a very intense reaction to the tragedy that befell her and millions of other people. She understands the words Albrecht Goes wrote in *Das Brandopher*:

Yet there comes a time for forgetting,
for who could live and not forget?
Now and then, however, there must also
be one who remembers.

Daniel Jonah Goldhagen has written an important book in which he posits the view that Adolf Hitler did not act alone. In *Hitler's Willing Executioners—Ordinary Germans and the Holocaust*, Goldhagen goes into great detail to trace the persistence of anti-Semitism throughout European, and especially German history, and makes a case for the widespread participation of the masses. "My explanation," he writes, "which is new to the scholarly literature on the perpetrators—is that the perpetrators, 'ordinary Germans,' were animated by anti-Semitism, by a particular type of anti-Semitism that led them to conclude that the Jews ought to die. The perpetrators' beliefs, their particular brand of anti-Semitism, though obviously not the sole source, was, I maintain, a most significant and indispensable source of the perpetrators' actions and must be at the center of any explanation of them. Simply put, the perpetrators, having consulted their own convictions and morality and having judged the mass annihilation of Jews to be right, did not want to say no."

Goldhagen charts the course of Nazi persecution of Jews from emigration and deportations to slave labor camps and the furnaces where they were "strung up, trampled underfoot, bitten by trained dogs, whipped, and humiliated in every conceivable manner." Jew-hatred was so deeply embedded in the culture that the total extermination of human beings considered to be sub-human was accepted as normative, even necessary. In explaining why he killed Jews, Rudolf Hess, commandant of Auschwitz, said, "You can be sure that it was not always a pleasure to see those mountains of corpses and smell the continual burning, but Himmler had ordered it and had even explained the necessity of it and I really never gave much thought to whether it was wrong. It just seemed necessary."

Thousands of Jews fled the country in droves, choosing to go to any country that would admit them. Dispossessed of their livelihoods, virtually turned into social dead beings, they forfeited their property, belongings and wealth. Other thousands were dispatched to conquered areas of the Soviet Union where many were massacred. Of the half million Jews living in Germany in 1933, almost 140,000 emigrated during the next five years. Some were able to flee after the war began, but the Nazi goal was a Germany *judenrein*, free of Jews. Totally free.

Crystal Night was a turning point, an event of enormous significance. On the night of November 9, 1939, Germans in cities and towns across the country were awakened by the sound of breaking glass, the sight and smell of burning synagogues and the cries of Jews being raped and beaten by their countrymen. It was "the night of broken glass." The scope of the violence and destruction is reflected in the statistics: approximately a hundred Jews killed, thirty thousand or more hauled off to concentration camps, hundreds of synagogues burned and demolished, the storefront glass of 7,500 Jewish shops and businesses shattered, with damaged estimated in the hundreds of millions of Reichmarks.

Did German people react? Well, yes. But their criticism, even sometimes outrage, was short-sighted and self-centered. Many abhorred the violence, but some non-Jewish Germans wondered whether this kind of thing might turn on them. And might the Jews in the future revenge themselves upon Germany? Finally, they simply deplored the destruction of property. So much for any hint of sympathy or compassion for the victims of the savagery.

This was a pivotal moment in the march toward war. "The Third Reich had deliberately turned down a dark and savage road from which there was to be no return." Jews had been victimized by unruly street gangs before, robbed, tortured, murdered, but this was the first time the German government had organized and carried out such a terror. As Alfons Heck, an erstwhile member of the Hitler Youth, put it, "after *Kristallnacht*, no German old enough to walk could ever plead ignorance of the persecution of the Jews, and no Jews could harbor any delusion that Hitler wanted Germany anything but *judenrein*, free of Jews.

A hundred thousand people crowded into a rally at Nuremberg the day after the nationwide orgy that shocked the world, and photographs show relatively few men in uniform. It was ordinary Germans, celebrating the breaching of civilized roadblocks, egged on by the vulgar and violent SA gangs, and this time, with the consent and encouragement of the government. "This, perhaps the most revealing day of the entire Nazi era," Goldhagen asserts, "the day on which an opportunity presented itself for the German people to rise up in solidarity with fellow citizens, was the day on which the German people sealed the fate of the Jews, by letting the authorities know that they concurred in the unfolding eliminationist enterprise, even if they objected, sometimes vociferously, to some of its measures."

The policies that the Germans subsequently implemented were articulated by *Das Schwarze Korps* two weeks after this nationwide outbreak of violence. "The Jews must be driven from our residential districts and segregated where they will be among themselves, having as little contact with Germans possible. Confined to themselves, these parasites will be reduced to poverty.

There was to be a next stage. The editorial continued: "Let no one fancy, however, that we shall then stand idly by, merely watching the process. The German people are not in the least inclined to tolerate in their country hundreds of thousands of criminals, who not only secure their existence through crime, but also want to exact revenge. In such a situation we would be faced with the hard necessity of exterminating the Jewish underworld in the same way as, under our government of law and order, we are accustomed to exterminating any other criminals—that is, by fire and sword. The result would be the actual and final end of Jewry in Germany, its absolute annihilation."

Emigration, deportations, ship them out of the country. Isolate the remaining undesirables, these criminals, shove them into ghettos, remove them from the good people. Fine them, eliminate them from the economy, rob them of everything they possess. "German Jewry shall, as punishment for their abominable crimes, have to make a contribution of one billion marks," Hermann Goering yells at a meeting called to solve the Jewish question. "That will work. The swine won't commit another murder. Incidentally, I would like to say that I would not like to be a Jew in Germany."

But these measures alone would not suffice to satisfy the sadistic appetites of the monsters who had taken over the reins of the Third Reich. How many times has it been noted that the anti-Semitism propelling this country to a disaster unparalleled in history is beyond comprehension? Even when "reasons" and explanations are advanced, we are left to wonder. For example, the Jews must suffer. It is not enough that they die; while alive, they must be punished, degraded. "The unwritten commandment to beat Jews, to mock them, to make their lives miserable was at the root of the Germans' pervasive cruelty." And so the pace of mistreatment and persecution moves toward elimination. En route toward the pits, the work camps and the gas chambers, "the Germans debased and inflicted pain upon Jews with a regularity calculated not just to cripple their bodies but also to plunge them into a state of perpetual terror."

If descriptions of the measures devised to commit genocide, to destroy a people whose lives are "unworthy of living," take one's breath away, picture yourself at the scene in August 1941.

Heinrich Himmler, Gestapo chief, traveled to Minsk where he personally witnessed a hundred Jews being shot in a ditch outside the town. The event is described by SS-Oberguppenfuhrer Karl Wolf in his diary, "Himmler's face was green. He took out his handkerchief and wiped his cheek where a piece of brain had squirted upon it. Then he vomited. After he recovered his composure, he lectured the SS men on the need to follow 'the highest moral law of the party' in carrying out their tasks."

In the evolution of the eliminationist program, someone came up with the idea of simply shooting and burying Jews. Hapless victims, marched out of the ghettos, were forced to dig their own graves. One such pit was about 150 meters long, 30 meters wide and a good 15 meters deep. When they reached the bottom of the ravine, having removed their luggage, coats and shoes, their outer garments and even underwear, they were seized by members of the Schutzpolizei, made to lie down on top of Jews who had already been shot. A marksman came along and shot each Jew in the neck with a submachine gun.

The world watched in horror as the best educated and one of the most cultivated nations in Europe spiraled out of control. Civilized people everywhere recoiled as they witnessed the German nation in freefall. The murderous engine of racism barreled down the tracks, absent of restraint, fueled by a hatred that knew no bounds, a hatred that in too many cases was shared by the man on the street, the "ordinary" German.

Man's inhumanity to his fellow creatures reached its nadir in the camps, detention camps, "work" camps, and extermination centers known as "death factories." Each camp had its own personality, bore its own stigma. Dachau and Buchenwald, among the most notorious, were the first camps established soon after Hitler came to power in 1933. They were set up primarily as places of detention for political prisoners and other "criminals," Jews and non-Jews alike. When the gates of Dachau were flung open at liberation, General Eisenhower and other witnesses were stunned and angered at what they saw. In Buchennwald, whose infamy will live forever, SS men were seen throwing children into the flames alive. In his famous 1945 broadcast from the camp, Edward R. Murrow said, "There surged around me an evil-smelling horde. Men and boys reached out to touch me; they were in rags and the remnants of uniform. Death had already marked many of them, but they were smiling with their eyes."

It was in Chelmno that the first mass killings of Jews by gas took place. Located in a small village near Lodz, the camp executed 150,000 to 300,000 Jews in gas vans using carbon monoxide. It was a clean operation, but only a foretaste of the sheer and evil brilliance of German technology to be perfected by the murderers of Treblinka and Auschwitz, where millions were consumed in the ovens.

The boast of Treblinka was "from door to door in forty-five minutes." Twenty thousand human beings could be "processed" each day—"from opening the cattle cars to slamming shut the gas chambers." Treblinka was designed for one thing only: dispose of as many Jews as possible, as quickly as possible. Nearly a million Jews died at Treblinka before August 22, 1943. "On that day," the Los Angeles Times reports, "600 prisoners armed with stolen guns and grenades attacked the Nazi guards, burned the camp, and fled into the nearby Polish forests. Of these, forty survived to bear witness to man's courage in the face of the greatest evil human history has provided."

Scores of such camps had sprung up across Europe. Although thousands of inmates died from beating and starvation, from random killing and exhaustion and epidemics, most of these camps were not designed as instruments of genocide. There were six great "killing centers," as they began to be called: Auschwitz-Burkenau, Sobibor, Chelmno, Belzer, Maidanaek, and Treblinka; and it is interesting to note that none of them is located in the Reich—"as if in this way the Germans could indulge in atrocities without tainting German soil and thus, by some mad logic, remain pure and remote from their own evil."

Fifty to seventy people died at a time in Chelmno's gas vans. Twenty thousand a day perished at Treblinka: "from door to door in forty-five minutes." By the time you reach Auschwitz, hell has enlarged its borders . Mass murder has been reduced to a fine science. A worker said that the stench given off by the pyres contaminated the surrounding countryside. At night the red sky over Auschwitz could be seen for miles.

Welcome to Auschwitz, the greatest human extermination center of all time; "the black hole of history," as Elie Wiesel called it. To simply visualize it is mind-numbing: "Dr. Mengele, immaculate in his SS uniform, standing before endless columns of people on a railway ramp, slowly moving a finger of his glove hand to the right (death), to the left (temporary left), a judge more almighty than God."

This is Auschwitz-Burkenau, actually a series of camps, located in the southwestern corner of Poland near the Czech border. Rudolf Hess, the commandant, bears direct responsibility for "the mass murders committed on a scale unknown in history." Hess was well qualified for the job, a psychopath by anybody's definition, who had spent five years in prison for murder. He claimed to have no personal animosity toward the Jews. "I must emphasize," he wrote from his Polish prison after the war, shortly before he was hanged, "I have never personally hated the Jews. It is true that I looked upon them as enemies of our people, but the emotion of hatred is so foreign to me."

Stepping over mounds of corpses, enduring the smell of burning flesh, dealing with recalcitrant prisoners, was not the most pleasant thing; but it was all in a day's work. And the pay was pretty good. The Hess family lived well in a large, comfortable home just a stone's throw beyond barded wire fences, police dogs, SS guards keeping order with leather whips—and the furnaces.

"My family, to be sure, were well provided for in Auschwitz," Hess wrote. "Every wish that my wife or children expressed was granted them. The children could live a free and untrammeled life. My wife's garden was a paradise of flowers." Mrs. Hess corroborated the statement and often said, "I want to live here till I die" Caterers provided food and wine, prisoners worked in the garden, and the Hess children wore the clothing of other children who had been murdered by their father.

Traumatized and terrorized men, women and children, arriving by cattle car by day and by night, did not associate their plight with paradise. They were greeted by SS-Hauptsturmfuhrer Fritzsch, camp leader: You have come to a Gerrman concentration camp, not to a sanatorium, and there is only one way out—through the chimney. Anyone who does not like it can try hanging himself on the wires. If there are Jews in this draft, they have no right to live longer than a fortnight; if there are priests, their period is one month—the rest, three months."

Seventy-plus years after Fritzsch's welcome to Auschwitz, visitors come to walk the haunted paths and alleyways of the camp, silent and pensive. There is the wall against which they lined up prisoners to be shot, there the gallows where men, even boys, no longer "fit to live" were hanged. Down the stairs on the wooden table in the corner room Dr. Joseph Mengele performed experiments on living human beings, including many children. Behind a glass in one of the buildings are mounds of hair from the heads of pretty Jewish girls. In another room are thousands of pairs of shoes once proudly worn by little children. Stacks of luggage bear mute testimony to the arrival of travelers whose journey abruptly ended here.

Then there are the gas chambers. Men were separated from the women. Prisoners were taken to dressing rooms, where they were instructed to leave their clothes, so they could find them readily after they had been bathed and deloused. The deception and meanness never ended.

Commandant Hess described the procedure: "Women went in first with their children. The doors were then sealed and gas shaken down through holes in the roof. For a little while a humming sound could be heard, then cries of 'Gas!' Then a great bellowing and the trapped prisoners hurled themselves against the doors."

"One woman approached me," Hess remembered, "and as she walked past, pointing to her four children, whispered, 'How can you bring yourself to kill such beautiful, darling children? Have you no heart at all?'"

A distinguished rabbi recently arrived from France, after undressing, approached Hess, and taking hold of the lapels of his uniform, said, "You common, cruel murderers of mankind, do not think you will succeed in extinguishing our nation. The Jewish nation will live forever and will not disappear from the world's arena."

Following the killing, the doors were opened and the corpses lifted and placed in the oven. The ashes were taken to the Vistula where they drifted and dissolved.

After the camps were liberated, witnesses confirmed that Nina Altmon's mother and little sister Helen went first to the gas chamber while her father watched, then followed. Unless one was there, who can speak for the victims, whose agony to this day is visible in the millions of scratches made by fingernails on the ceilings of gas chambers?

One understands the sentiment of Elie Wiesel, whose family disappeared in the ovens: "My gaze stops at the gas chambers. Even in thought, I refuse to violate the privacy of the victims at the moment of their death." Our gaze stops as this chapter closes, benumbed by the painful rehearsal of the events of those days when hell was in session.

12

Marching to Zion

A patriot is defined as a person who loves, supports, and defends his or her country and its interests. General Pinkney, one of the delegates to the Constitutional Convention in 1787, said, "If I had a vein which did not beat with the love of my country, I myself would open it." Euripides wrote, "There is no greater sorrow on earth than the loss of one's native land."

But are we losing our native land? If you listened to country singer Merle Haggard, the tumultuous decade of the Sixties "was just the evening of it all; I think we're into the dead of night now." We have in these pages identified and examined some of the spiritual and cultural indicators of our time which seem to suggest that Mr. Haggard may have called it right.

The truth is that nations die. Look at ancient Carthage, six hundred years before the birth of Christ. It's hard to imagine the wealth and power that once existed here; now nothing but desolation and ruin—and across the Mediterranean and six hundred miles to the west , the ancient ports of Spain: Cadiz, Malaga, Almeria, Cartegena, Alicante, and Barcelona. The architecture, language, the traditions remain, but the glory is gone. In the last century we witnessed the fall of the German Reich, the Austro-Hungarian Empire, the Italian Empire of Benito Mussolini, Hirohito's Japan, and even the Great British Empire. Some of us learned in the fifth grade that "the sun never sets on the British Empire." Remember that one? The truth is that history is cluttered with the remains of ancient empires.

What causes certain societies to rise so high and then collapse, some so suddenly? What are the signs of the impending death of a nation? Among the social symptoms we should recognize are increased lawlessness, loss of economic discipline and self-restraint, rising bureaucracy, loss of respect for established religion. Sound familiar? William Bennett says, "There is a coarseness, callousness, and cynicism, a banality and a vulgarity to our time. There are just too many signs of decivilization: that is, civilization gone rotten." As Russell Kirk has said, the roots of "culture" come from the "cult"—that is, the religious beliefs upon which societies are founded. Every society is based on some kind of cult-ure and upon some form of religious and spiritual worldview. When those beliefs are eroded, the nation dies. History bears this out. Will Durant notes, "There is no significant example in history, before our time, of a society successfully maintaining moral life without the aid of religion."

Are we living through the twilight of a great civilization or could a sweeping moral and spiritual revival stop hell in its path and turn our nation back to God? It is long past time that the church of Jesus Christ rediscovers the old-fashioned prayer meeting, where the people of God gather—and linger—to implore heaven for national righteousness, for spiritual renewal of the church as well as the salvation of the lost. In chapter nine of the Book of Daniel, the prophet and statesman confesses before God the sins of his nation. He identifies himself with the people and stands in the gap for them. So must we. The African antelope called the gnu has an interesting characteristic. When attacked, it kneels and returns the attack from its knees. As the dark night settles upon us, the church could do no better than to wage spiritual warfare on its knees, engaging in effectual, fervent prayer. No better strategy can be found, when all else fails, than to "kneel down and be counted."

It cannot be denied that the Wesleyan revival spared England a blood bath similar to that which tore the heart out of France during the French Revolution. That great spiritual awakening also led to the enactment of much-needed child labor laws and prison reform. When our young nation was threatened by unbelief and apostasy in the eighteenth century, a move of the Spirit of God stanched the hemorrhaging and brought us back to our senses. Every revival that has taken place in history has had three parts: a call to repentance, a renewal of the Holy Spirit's working in individual personal lives, and social change.

Desperately do we need that kind of dynamic intervention. "Sin is terribly funny to the American people," writes Roy T. Edgemon. "We are giggling and laughing our way straight to hell. There is a cynicism about integrity—from the White House to Capitol Hill, to the county court house and backyard fence." Will Durant wrote something in the last century that is particularly appropriate for this century. The philosopher stated, "The greatest question of our time is whether humans can bear to live without God. Can a civilization hold together if man abandons his faith in God?" Christopher Frye wrote in *The Lady's Not for Burning*, "I've never seen a world so festering with damnation."

One of the reasons for this "festering with damnation" characterizing our age is the loss of any sense of accountability, of a day of reckoning. Florida pastor Charles W. Keysor wonders, "What has become of eternity? Like a recurring theme in a composition by Beethoven or Bach, eternity is an integral theme for all humanity." The pastor reminds us:

> Death awaits each of us. What then? Will we simply cease to exist, like spots washed out of a dirty shirt? Or is there another life waiting for us "out there" after we have passed through the experience of dying? Eternity cannot be avoided or evaded. The Bible makes it clear that eternity has already enveloped us, that as we live this present life we are already traversing the foothills of eternity, foothills which lead each human being to a never-ending destiny either with God or apart from Him.

We've stripped heaven and hell of their eternal dimension. Keysor says, "One might presume that a consciousness of eternity would pervade the church's ministry to people of all ages and conditions of life. This assumption would have been quite true in years past. No longer!"

Martin Marty, eminent church historian from the University of Chicago, remarks, "The passing of hell from modern consciousness is one of the modern trends of our time." One would think that times like these would elicit some seriousness from men who are never more than one borrowed breath away from eternity—but one is often wrong. My naivete may be showing, but I thought we were past the sophomoric silliness one used to hear, but there it was this week in a blog. After the writer gave his reasons for dismissing God from his thoughts, he said, "If that sends one to hell, at least I'll be there with a lot of my favorite people." Men can afford the luxury of foolish talk when they no longer believe in eternity, when there is no fear of God before their eyes.

The need is urgent for a generation of preachers who can identify with John Wesley who often spoke of himself as a "brand plucked from the burning." In a letter to John Smith dated June

25, 1746, Wesley wrote, "I desire to have both heaven and hell ever in my eye, while I stand on this isthmus of life between these two boundless oceans; and I verily think the daily consideration of both highly becomes all men of reason and religion." What is needed is a pervasive biblical awareness of eternity, without which not much is likely to happen in our churches or in our land.

The late Carl F. H. Henry, one of America's foremost theologians, said, "If we are to shape an evangelical counterculture, it must start in the church, in prayer meetings, in members turning out by the hundreds and thousands and tens of thousands seeking renewal, in so many cars suddenly parked near a local church that the world once again becomes curious about what is taking place in those forsaken sanctuaries, and give credence to the rumor that God is alive in the history of our times." Then Dr. Henry makes an impassioned plea: "Let the restoration of the prayer meeting be the mirror of a rising evangelical counterculture."

But what if the people do not pray and there is no revival? What if there is no moral and spiritual resurgence and our country continues its downward spiral toward lawlessness? On one of his first visits to Great Britain, Billy Graham met with Winston Churchill. "Do you have any hope, young man?" the prime minister asked the American evangelist.

Do you have any hope, a weary world asks. What of the future—or is there a future? Perhaps it's time for some straight talk. God never promised that America would live forever. Times are bad, but they've always been bad, but He "who abolished death and brought life and immortality to light through the gospel" is at the right hand of God. America may not survive; civilizations crumble and nations die, but as far as heaven is concerned nothing has changed; the grave is still empty and the heavens declare the glory of God.

Our ultimate hope does not rest in stars and stripes but in the promise of a carpenter's Son who said, "My kingdom is not of this world." America may not survive, but Jesus will. And was there not something strange about this Nazarene who said He had come from God and was going to God? What did He mean by that? He spoke of a kingdom, but he didn't look like a king, wandering around Galilee with a shabby entourage of fishermen and tax collectors. This "king" had no place to lay His head, never rode in a limousine. His only conveyance was a donkey. He seldom hobnobbed with the uptown crowd, choosing rather to mingle with publicans and sinners. Oh, he did meet once with a powerful governor, but that resulted in a brutal beating and crucifixion on a Roman cross.

Of course we love our country; that's what this story is about. Hence our concern for her welfare. It is appropriate to love one's native land. The people of God are salt and light in the community. We are commanded to pray for those in authority— but national sovereignties are not forever. When life's little day is ended and the curtains fall and they turn out the lights, when everything that can be shaken is shaken; when the last page is written and they close the books, every knee shall bow and every tongue confess that Jesus is Lord.

Do we have any hope? Russell Moore writes in his important book, *Onward*: "The worst thing that could happen to us has already happened: we're dead, we were crucified with Him. And the best thing that could happen to us has already happened: we're alive in Christ." Then Moore assures us: "We will overcome, not because we're a moral majority but because we're sinners saved by grace."

Are we discouraged? Not here, not now, not ever, because "The arc of history is long, but it bends toward Jesus." We're marching to Zion.

AS CHRISTIANS, we know that in this world we have no continuing city, that crowns roll in the dust and that every earthly king must sometime flounder—We acknowledge a King that men did not crown and cannot dethrone, and we are citizens of a city of God they did not build and cannot destroy.

Malcolm Muggeridge

Notes

FOREWORD

Charles A. Beard, Mary A. Beard, *New Basic History of the United States* (Doubleday & Co., Inc., Garden City, NY, 1960).

Alexis de Tocqueville, *Democracy in America*, (New American Library, New York, NY, 1956).

WE THE PEOPLE

Rabbi Daniel Lapin, *America's Real War* (Multnomah Publishers, Sister, OR, 1999).
Barack Obama, (Turkish Press Conference, April 6, 2009).
Catherine Drinker Bowen, *Miracle at Philadelphia*, (Little, Brown & Co., Boston, Toronto, 1966).
Alexis de Tocqueville, *Democracy in America* (New American Library, New York, NY,
Russell Kirk, *The Roots of American Order* (Regnery Gateway, Washington, D.C., 1991).
Bradley Project on American Identity, 2008
Balint Vazonyi, *America's 30 Years War* (Regnery Publishing Co., Washington, D.C. 1998).
Thomas Oden, *After Modernity* (Zondervan Publishing House, Grand Rapids, MI., 1992).

THE UNBREAKABLE COVENENT

Dennis Prager and Joseph Telushkin, (Touchstone, 2003).
Golda Meir, *My Life* (G.P. Putnam's Sons, New York, NY, 1975).

TRUTH OR CONSEQUENCES

Charles Darwin, *Origen of Species*, 1959.
William L. Shirer, *The Rise and Fall of the Third Reich* (Simon & Schuster, New York, NY, 1959)
Richard Terrell, *Ressurecting the Third Reich* (Huntington House Publishers, 1994).
Albert Speed, Inside the Third Reich.
Richard M. Weaver, *Ideas Have Consequences*, (University Press, Chicago, IL, 1948).

WHY JOHNNY CAN'T READ

Henry Steele Commager, *The American Mind* (Yale Publishing, New Haven & London, 1950).
Pierre DuPont de Nemours, *Education in the United States* (University of Delaware Press, Newark, DE, 1923).
Karl Shapiro, speaking to California Library Association, 1970.
George S. Counts, *Dare the School Build a New Social Order*
Samuel Blumenfeld, *Trojan Horse in American Education*, (Paradigm Co., Boise, ID, 1994).
Ari Goldman, *The Search for God at Harvard* (Random House Publishing Group, New York, NY, 1991 & 2008).
Bernard A. Weisberger, *They Gathered at the River* (Little, Brown and Co., 1958)
Samuel Blumenfeld, Is *Public Education Necessary?* (Devin-Adair, 1981).
Richard Rorty, *Contingency, Iron, Solidarity* (Cambridge University Press, 1989).

BROKEN CISTERNS

Franklin P. Cole, *They Preached Liberty* (Coral Ridge Ministries, T. Lauderdale, FL).
Balint Vazonyi, *America's 30 Years War.*

R.C. Sproul, *Lifeviews* (Fleming H. Revell, Grand Rapids, MI, 1986).

Henning Webb Prentis, speaking, National Conference Board, 1943.

Cynthia Eagle Russett, Darwin in America (S.H. Freeman & Co., San Franscisco, 1976).

Dinesh D'Sousa, *What's So Great About America* (Regnery Publishing Inc., Washington, D.C., 2002).

THE SIXTIES AND BEYOND

Cal Thomas, columnist, *Imprimis*, Hillsdale College.
David Broder, columnist, *Imprimis*, Hillsdale College.
Thomas Babbngton Macaulay, letter to friend.
Robert Bork, *Slouching Towards Gommorah* (HarperCollins Publishers, 1996).

AS THE CHURCH GOES

Garry Wills, *Under God* (Simon Schuster, New York, NY, 1990).
Henry Steele Commager, *The American Mind* (The Alpine Press, Stoughton, MA, 1950).

LOST IN THE TEMPLE

Harold Lindsell, *The Battle for the Bible* (Zondervan Publishing Co., Grand Rapids, MI, 1976).

ARE WE YET ALIVE?

James Hitchcock, *What is Secular Humanism*? (RC Books, Harrison, New York, 1982).
Richard W. Halverson, *The Timelessness of Jesus Christ* (Regal Books, Ventura, CA, 1982)
Roy T. Edgemon, *Citizen Christians* (Broadman & Holmes Pub-

lishers, Nashville, TN, 1994).
WHEN THE CHURCH WAS SILENT

Judah Pilch, *The World Was Silen.t*
Margaret MacMillian, *Paris 1919* (Random House, New York, NY, 2003).

MARCHING TO ZION

Carl F.H. Henry, *Citizen Christians* (Broadman & Holmes Publishers, Nashville, TN, 1994)
Russell Moore, *Onward*, (B &H Publishing Group, 2015).

Suggested Reading

Postmodern Times, Gene Edward Veith, Jr.: Crossway Books, Wheaton, IL, 1994.

After Modernity, Thomas C. Oden: Zondervan Publishing House, 1990.

Impossible People, Os Guinness InterVarsity Press, Downers Grove, IL 2016.

Onward, Russell Moore: B & H Publishing Group, Nashville, TN 2015.

The Dust of Death, Os Guinness: InterVarsity Press, Downers Grove, IL, 1973.

Paris 1919, Margaret MacMillan: Random House, New York, NY, 2001.

When Nations Die, Jim Nelson Black: Tyndale House Publishers, Wheaton, IL, 1994.

Hitler's Cross: Erwin W. Lutzer, Moody Press, Chicago, IL, 1995.

The Bible Jesus Read, Phillip Yancey: Harper Collins, Zondervan Publishing Co., Grand Rapids, MI, 1999.

The New Absolutes, William D. Watkins: Bethany House Publishers, Minneapolis, MN, 1996.

Total Truth, Nancy Pearcey: Crossway Books, Wheaton, IL, 2004.

Resurrecting the Third Reich, Richard Terrell: Huntington House Publishers, Lafayette, LA, 1994.

America's 30 Years War, Balint Vazsonyi: Regnery Publishing, Inc., Washington, D.C., 1998.

The Closing of the American Heart, Ronald H. Nash: Probe Books, USA, 1990.

And Are We Yet Alive, Richard B. Wilke: Abingdon Press, Nashville, TN 1986.

The Sword of the Prophet, Serge Trifkovic: Regina Orthodox Press, Boston, MA, 2002.
Darwin in America, Cynthia Eagle Russett: W. H. Freeman & Co., San Francisco, CA, 1976.

What is Secular Humanism? James Hitchcock: R. C. Books, Harrison, NY, 1982.

Castings From the Foundry Mold, Homer L. Calkin: Parthenon Press, Nashville, TN, 1968.

What's So Great About America, Dinesh D'Souza: Regnery Publishing, Inc., Washington D. C. 2002.

American Exceptionalism, Seymour Martin Lipset: W. W. Norton & Co., New York, London, 1996.

The Battle for the Bible, Harold Lindsell: Zondervan Publishing Co., Grand Rapids, MI, 1976.

Abortion—Toward an Evangelical Consensus, Paul B. Fowler: Multnomah, Portland, OR, 1987.

Absolute Confusion, George Barna: Regal Books, Ventura, CA, 1993.

The Adams Family, James Truslow Adams: Blue Ribbon Books, NY, 1930.

America: To Pray or Not to Pray, David Barton: Aledo, TX, 1988.

American Historial Documents, Harvard Classics: Grolier Enterprises, Corp., Danbury, CT, 1980.

American History Before1877, Ray A. Billington: Littlefield, Adams & Co., Totowa, NJ, 1965.

The American Mind, Henry Steel Commager: Yale University Press, New Haven & London, 1950.

A Basic History of the U. S., Clarence B. Carson: American Textbook Committee, 1994.

Builders of the Bay Colony, Samuel Eliot Morison: Northeastern University, Boston, MA, 1930.

Bulwark of the Republic, Benton J. Hendrick: Little, Brown & Bo., Boston, MA, 1937.

The Christian History of the Constitution of the United States of America, Joseph Allan Montgomery: Foundation for American Christian Education, San Francisco, CA, 1966.

Classics of Protestantism, Vergilius Ferm, editor: Philosophical Library, New York, NY, 1959.

A Christian Manifesto, Francis Schaeffer: Crossway Books, Wheaton, IL, 1981.

The Closing of the American Mind, Allan Bloom: Simon & Schuster, New York, NY, 1989.

The Creation of the American Republic, 1776-1787, Gordon S. Wood: University of North Carolina Press, Chapel Hill, SC, 1969.

The Cry of the Innocents, John O. Anderson: Bridge Publishing, South Plainfield, NJ, 1984.

The Culture of Disbelief, Stephen Carter: Basic Books, New York, NY, 1993.

A Dance With Death, Charles Colson: Word Publishers, Callas, TX, 1993.

The Day America Told the Truth, James Patterson and Peter Kimm: Prentice Hall Press, New York, NY, 1991.

Democracy in America, Alexis de Tocqueville: Mentor Books, New York, NY, 1956.

The Devaluing of America, William J. Bennett: Simon & Schuster, New York, NY, 1992.

Faith of Our Founding Fathers, Tim LaHaye: Wolgemuth & Hyatt, Brentwood, TN, 1987.

The Fall of the Ivory Tower, George Roche: Regnery Publishers, Washington, D. C., 1994.

A History of Colonial America, Max Sanelle & Robert Middekauff: Holt, Rinehart & Winston, New York, NY, 1964.

The Five Thousand Year Leap, W. Cleon Skousen: National

Center for Constitutional Studies, Washington, D. C., 1981.

Inventing America, Garry Wills: Doubleday, Garden City, NY, 1978.

Jefferson, Albert Jay Nack: Harcourt, Brace & Co., Rahway, NY, 1926.

New Basic History of the U. S., Charles A. & Mary R. Beard: Doubleday, Garden City, NY, 1944.

A Nation at Risk: the National Commission of Excellence in Education, 1983.

Miracle at Philadelphia, Catherine Drinker Bowen: Little, Brown & Co., Boston, MA, 1966.

The Living U. S. Constitution, Saul K. Padover: New American Library, New York, NY, 1983.

Lives and Graves of our Presidents, G. S. Weaver: Elder Publishing Co., Chicago, IL, 1984.

Jonathan Edwards, the Preacher, Ralph Turnbull: Baker Book House, Grand Rapids, MI, 1958.

Religion in American Public Life, A. James Reichley: The Brookings Institution, Washington, D. C., 1985.

The Return of the Puritans, Patricia O. Brooks: Whitaker House, Springdale, PA, 1976.

Religious Apartheid, John W. Whitehead: Moody Press, Chicago, IL, 1994.

The Rewriting of America's History, Catherine Millard: Horizon House, Camp Hill, PA, 1991.

The Roots of American Order, Russell Kirk: Regnery Gateway, Washington, D. C., 1991.

The Rise and Fall of the Third Reich, William L. Shirer: Simon & Schuster, New York, NY, 1960.

The Rockets Red Glare, Richard J. Barnet: Simon & Schuster, New York, NY, 1990.

School Choice, David Harmer: Cato Institute, Washington, D. C., 1994.

They Gathered at the River, Bernard A. Weisberger: Quadrangel Paperbacks, Chicago, IL, 1966.

This Freedom, Whence, J. Wesley Bready: American Tract Society, New York, NY, 1946.

Whatever Became of Sin, Karl Menninger: Bantam Books, Toronto, New York, NY, 1985.

Under God: Religion and American Politics, Garry Wills: Simon & Schuster, New York, NY, 1990.

The Timelessness of Jesus Christ: His Relevance in Today's World, Richard C. Halverson, Regal Books, Ventura, CA, 1982.

What Are They Teaching Our Children, Mel and Norma Gabler: Victor Books, Wheaton, IL, 1985.

When the Wicked Seized the City, Chuck and Donna Mclheny: Huntington House, Lafayette, IN, 1993.

About the Author

Daniel E. Johnson (Dan Johnson Sr.) president of Trans World Ministries, an author and speaker, comes from a long line of preachers including his father and three brothers. He grew up in North Dakota where his father was a pioneer preacher and first superintendent of the Assemblies of God in North Dakota.

A student of history and cultural trends, after pastoring for thirty years, Dan has devoted himself to study and research, writing and speaking on the role of the people of God in the life of our nation. He is the author or editor of eight books and numerous articles, and has appeared on TBN, Daystar, and numerous television and radio stations. He was a member of the advisory committee sponsored by the Billy Graham Evangelistic Association and served as a representative of Teen Challenge.

Dan continues to travel widely, speaking in churches and schools. Pastor Ralph Snook, Vineland, New Jersey, said, "Listening to Dan Johnson was the first time I had ever heard Dr. Criswell, Winston Churchill and Woody Allen quoted in the same sermon."

Paul Jardin, Former mayor of Green Bay, Wisconsin, said "I have enjoyed your books in which you so ably identified our nation's denial of God and gradual descent from family structure."

Dr. Des Evans commented, "As the author of Come Home America, Dan Johnson provokes even the most conscientious Christian. His motivation is love for this nation and a desire that her children find life in Jesus instead of death in the jungle of mangled morality."

Dan and his wife Martha have three children and live in Memphis, Tennessee.